Clumsy Love

A Father's Journey Parenting
His Transgender Daughter

A Memoir

Andrew Patrie

LITTLE CREEK PRESS
MINERAL POINT, WISCONSIN

Copyright © 2025 Andrew Patrie

All rights reserved. No part of this publication may be reproduced, distributed, or transmitted in any form or by any means, including photocopying, recording, digital scanning, or other electronic or mechanical methods, without the prior written permission of the publisher, except in the case of brief quotations embodied in critical reviews and certain other noncommercial uses permitted by copyright law. For permission requests or other information, please send correspondence to the following address:

Little Creek Press
5341 Sunny Ridge Road
Mineral Point, WI 53565

ORDERING INFORMATION
Quantity sales. Special discounts are available on quantity purchases by corporations, associations, and others. For details, contact info@littlecreekpress.com

Orders by US trade bookstores and wholesalers.
Please contact Little Creek Press or Ingram for details.

Printed in the United States of America

Cataloging-in-Publication Data
Names: Andrew Patrie, author
Title: Clumsy Love
Description: Mineral Point, WI Little Creek Press, 2025
Identifiers: LCCN: 2025901878 | ISBN: 978-1-955656-92-4
Categories: FAMILY & RELATIONSHIPS / LGBTQ+
BIOGRAPHY & AUTOBIOGRAPHY / Memoirs
BIOGRAPHY & AUTOBIOGRAPHY / LGBTQ+

Book design by Little Creek Press

"Nature has introduced great variety
into the landscape, but man has displayed
a passion for simplifying it."

—Rachel Carson, *Silent Spring*

For Simone

FOREWORD

Growing up, nothing in my life felt quite right. From the khaki jeans and striped T-shirts I wore to the unease I felt every time I looked in the mirror, it was as if my mind and body weren't speaking the same language. By the time I was four, I started wondering if, somewhere in the process of my creation, the blueprints had been switched at the last minute—my brain and personality fully formed, but my body built differently. If I was a girl, why did I have the body of a boy?

It wasn't until I was nine that I realized I wasn't alone. As the word *transgender* flashed across cable news, a door opened, and I began to understand myself in a way I never had before. By age ten, I had already lived two versions of my life: first as Simon, a boy confused and trapped in a body that didn't fit, and then as Simone, a girl who refused to let the world define her.

Clumsy Love is the story of that journey—mine and my father's. There is no guidebook for parenting a transgender child, and my parents did their best to support me through love, trial, and error. Love, as this book reminds us, is often messy—but I never doubted that I was loved.

This book was made with literal love. My father shares these slices of our life with raw emotion, humor, and honesty. Once you start reading, you'll find it hard to stop. Though I lived many of these moments, hearing them through his perspective has been deeply healing. Reliving my life as Simon—something I avoided for so long—has helped me find closure, acceptance, and a deeper understanding of who I am today.

At a time when transgender youth are increasingly under attack, *Clumsy Love* carries even greater significance. May this book help destigmatize the transgender experience, remind the world of the humanity behind every identity, and ensure that these stories continue to be told.

As you navigate your own journey—however clumsily, as I did, as my father did, as we all do—I hope *Clumsy Love* brings you comfort. I hope it helps heal wounds, seen and unseen. I hope it reminds you that you are not alone, and that everyone deserves acceptance and love. Most of all, I hope this book makes you laugh, cry, and feel all the feels.

—Simone

CONTENTS

- Follow Your Path 1
- The Changeling 6
- The Kindness of Strangers 35
- Walker Between Worlds 41
- Checking In, Checking Out 54
- What Would You Do? 61
- Storm Warning 71
- A Proposal 83
- No Good Deed 94
- His or Hers 101
- Simone 109
- I Sing the Body Telekinetic 124
- Visiting Hours 144
- Dress Rehearsal 150
- Birds and Bees 155
- Escape Rooms 162
- On the Team 170
- Love Wins 176
- PSA on Behalf of GSA 189
- Seeds 197
- A Part of Rather Than Apart From 204
- Common Ground 210
- Escape Artists 219
- An Ending-Beginning 226
- Acknowledgments 232
- About the Author 235

FOLLOW YOUR PATH

"Quite a view today," I say to the top of my daughter Simone's head, her face pushed into the crumple of sweatshirt on the picnic table.

Her response is lost in a muffle of cotton.

We are at the University of Wisconsin. The Terrace is bustling with students and other people out enjoying the afternoon. The sky nearly cloudless and blue. We are lucky to have found a table so near the water of Lake Mendota. A rowing group glides by, a man with a megaphone perched like a gull at the stern. Closer, two bulldogs laze between the legs of their owners. The woman checks to see that the green leash is securely fastened to the back of her chair and looks our way, her eyes seeming to linger on Simone.

My wife, Adrienne, motions with her head: *Maybe we should go?*

I set down my cider and look to our daughter, still bowed over the table. The afternoon sun warms the nape of her neck between her parted hair.

Sure, I nod.

We walk parallel to the water, Adrienne and I several paces ahead while Simone lags behind. Nearby, ducks swim. I look back and catch Simone with arms raised, nose sniffing her armpits. I avert my eyes and look ahead instead, to spare us both embarrassment.

"She's nervous about tomorrow," I say.

"Totally nervous," Adrienne agrees. "Me, too."

We've arrived a day before our appointment to Madison to shop bookstores, eat pizza, swim at the hotel. To do the things Simone most enjoys in the hope of easing her mind.

And ours.

We wait for her to catch up. She almost walks into my back.

"We can talk about it," I say, "if you like."

Simone shakes her head and brushes past.

"It's okay to feel nervous," Adrienne calls.

Simone halts but does not turn.

"Are they going to poke me?" she asks.

"You mean draw your blood?" Adrienne asks.

Simone nods.

"I don't know," Adrienne says. "This is new for all of us."

Two years ago, our child informed us that she was our daughter, not our son. It has been a year since her name legally changed from the masculine to its feminine counterpart. Now May 2018, Simone is eleven, one summer away from middle school, and adamant she not go through male puberty. We've made an appointment at the Pediatric and Adolescent Transgender Health (PATH) Clinic in Madison, Wisconsin, to consult with an endocrinologist. The clinic is one of the few of its kind in the country, and we are fortunate it's only a three-hour drive from our home in Eau Claire.

The following morning we pile into the car and drive from the hotel to the PATH Clinic. When Google Maps directs us to take a right off University Avenue onto a road with no outlet, we believe we've been led astray. There is a gas station. Some train tracks. Adrienne and I look at each other. Think of those countless horror movies that begin with a fated wrong turn. Then we see a beige brick building slowly emerging beyond a leafy copse of trees. We park, stretch our legs, and head toward the lobby to check in. The receptionist sends us up a small set of marble stairs to the waiting room. We pull open the glass door and take a seat. Simone approaches the large aquarium in the center of the room, bending closer to watch the fish that fan out as if to make space for her.

Simone's name is called, and we follow a woman in blue scrubs to the doctor's office, find three chairs along the wall, and sit. Soon, there is a knock, and a cheerful voice behind the door says, "Hello. You must be Simone."

Our daughter nods.

The doctor enters. She has a cherubic face framed by close-cropped red hair and is wearing a petite white lab coat. No doubt a reassuring presence to scores of children. However, when she asks Simone the purpose of this visit, Simone is diffident, leaning toward Adrienne's ear and whispering for her to explain.

Adrienne says, "We wanted to go over puberty blockers. Simone is going to be twelve in a few months, and she's really worried the process has already begun."

The doctor focuses on Simone. "The good news is puberty doesn't happen all at once."

"I don't want any of it," Simone says.

"We can help with that," the doctor says, sitting down across from us.

"Are you going to draw my blood?" Simone asks.

"No," says the doctor as she grabs a blank sheet of paper and a pen from her desk. "But I'm gonna do a little drawing. Bear in mind, I'm not much of an artist, so no laughing."

Simone smiles as the doctor draws a crude body and an oversized head with a horizontal line running through it.

"Okay," the doctor continues, "this is your brain." Simone gives her first belly laugh of the trip. "Hey," the doctor says, "I told you no laughing." She pauses to grin and then continues, "Now, at the moment, your body is getting no message from your brain about puberty. But, when it does, the signal will look something like this." The doctor makes an exaggerated wavy line, like *The Outer Limits* logo. We lean toward the illustration like cave dwellers drawn to light. "What we can do is block the signal, return the line to horizontal." She explains how the drug disrupts the pubertal signal that would otherwise start in Simone's hypothalamus and then progress to her pituitary gland and finally her testes for production of the sex hormone testosterone.

"When would she start these blockers?" Adrienne asks.

The doctor turns to me and asks, "When did puberty start for you?"

"Um ..." Memories of boys showering after gym class superimpose themselves in the present. I look around the room at anatomy posters on the walls, still surprised my life has landed me in a place like this. "Later. Eighth grade, maybe?"

"Simone," the doctor says, "I'm guessing you'll be later, too. We'll need an X-ray of your hand to be sure." She explains how growth plates in Simone's fingers and wrist help determine bone age, which can be used to predict when puberty will begin.

Adrienne interjects, "How safe is all of this?"

"It's quite safe," the doctor says. "However, adding hormones later on raises the risk of sterility." She looks at Simone. "If you're thinking about having kids someday, you may want to consider allowing puberty to begin so you can harvest your sperm."

Unfazed, Simone replies, "I could just adopt. My dad was adopted."

I nod, though my brain is still catching up to this shift in conversation to our eleven-year-old and her fertility. My mom and dad struggled with infertility for years before they adopted me in 1975. Back then, fertility medicine was brand new. There was no in vitro fertilization (IVF) or harvesting of eggs and sperm. Even ultrasounds were not widely used. Men and boys who came out as women and girls, who knew in their bones they were born with the wrong genitals, were ostracized, often beaten—sometimes worse.

"I really don't want boy puberty," Simone says.

I clear my throat. "Well, it seems we have some things to discuss."

We follow single file to the elevator and take it to the basement for an X-ray of Simone's hand. The technician positions her and reminds her to relax. Moments later the segmented bones of her hand on film reveal its delicate construction and appear to glow beneath the skin. The doctor examines their growth and says she'd like to see Simone again in one year. It feels like borrowed time. We say our thanks, gather our things, and make our way to exit the clinic. Outside, as we cross the parking lot, Simone reaches for my hand. For the moment, at least, it still feels small.

THE CHANGELING

Before telling the story of how we came to parent our daughter, Simone, I must first tell the story of how we came to parent our son, Simon.

When Adrienne learned she was pregnant, we began pondering possible names. Collecting dust in a box somewhere in our basement is a copy of Bruce Lansky's *35,000+ Baby Names*. It was like scanning a menu when you're not sure what you're in the mood for: everything looked good; nothing looked good. Adrienne and I eventually agreed on "Winter" if our child was born a girl. Winter dominates almost half the calendar year in Wisconsin and possesses its own pleasing aesthetics: trees outlined in peppermint white, the filmic day-for-night blue of duskfall, time slowing to show the glinting of each dewy breath.

Naming proved more difficult when it came to a boy. Compounding the problem was the fact I was a teacher. My colleague Brian quipped, "As a teacher, most kid names have been ruined."

"Owen" had legs for a while until some friends stole it for their son. I said, "What about Simon?" The name had literary value. I had taught William Golding's *Lord of the Flies* for years. And in 2006, the spring before Simon was born, I wrote a critical analysis of the book in graduate school for a queer theory course. Contrary to traditional readings of the text, which placed the blame for the kids' crumbled island society on the character of Jack and his anarchy, I argued the culprit was actually the oft-valorized Ralph and his attempts to recreate on the island the status quo of the scorched world from whence they fled. In the undefined space of the tropical paradise upon which they are marooned, Jack sheds his prep school uniform of old and makes for himself a new identity out of the literal blood and clay of the island. However, Jack's liberation is ultimately squelched by the adults who come ashore at the novel's conclusion to "rescue" the kids and restore militaristic order. The paper was a radical departure in many ways, apart from its treatment of the "Simon" character. No matter the context or lens through which the book was viewed, he was always presented as this sweet kid, a tad eccentric yet comfortable in his own skin, a state of being the other boys were striving to achieve.

Simon was born September 20, 2006. That night a friend who came to visit at the hospital said something that echoed emphatically in my brain: *You'll never have a restful night's sleep again. The worry is infinite.*

Adrienne wanted a natural birth, but Simon contorted himself in such a way as to make that impossible. When the fetal monitor registered a pattern of distress, it was time for a Cesarean section. I stood in the operating room where Adrienne's head seemed to float, her body hidden behind a blue guillotine of curtain. The doctor was sure. The procedure was quick. Adrienne was fine. Soon a wailing, purple elfin-child was brought to me in the arms of a nurse. Days earlier, Adrienne had informed me of two post-labor and delivery tasks for me to complete: cut the umbilical cord, which I did, and change the first diaper. Simon complicated the latter by pooping while still in the womb. After I cut the cord, the nurse took Simon from us and rushed him to the Neonatal Intensive Care Unit (NICU), fearing he had aspirated meconium, his own fecal matter.

While the obstetrician stitched Adrienne back together, I was approached by the pediatrician overseeing the NICU. He was a trim man in his mid-thirties, some gray flecking his matte black beard. He put his hand on my shoulder. "We're going to take good care of Simon," he assured me. "What happened here isn't uncommon. However, it can lead to more serious complications."

I wanted to tell him how confused and desperate I felt. Instead, I said, "I understand."

"We'll bring him in for feedings," he said. "Otherwise, we'll keep him with us until we're sure he's in the clear."

"Thank you."

"Sure," he said. "Try and get some rest."

Between feedings, when they'd wheel Simon in so Adrienne could breastfeed, and while she continued to recover from surgery, I wandered the quiet hospital halls like a sleepwalker. Eventually, I found the NICU and my son's incubator. The nurse, seated at her station, looked up from her chart and smiled as I entered. I yawned, rubbed my eyes, and stared at Simon. He was on his back, naked but for a diaper, his eyes closed, his fists resting at each side of his head like two moons arrested now in orbit, a tiny, gold heart sticker affixed to a cardiac monitor on his chest, which seemed to pulse on its own but was only his breathing. I wondered at those lungs, if all that pink plumbing was clear now, if there was any scarring on his precious pipes.

The nurse on duty seemed to read my thoughts. She closed her chart and set it on the desk in front of her. "He's doing fine," she said. "I think we're past the point of concern."

I wondered if it was ever possible to pass such a point.

"So how much longer does he have to be in ... this?" I asked.

"I'd think this is the last night," she said.

I studied Simon: a latticework of blue ran under his skin, and his hair was the color of obsidian, not like mine or Adrienne's, but rather more like Adrienne's father. *Am I even there at all?* I thought. I imagined my birth mother looking in on me, seeking some semblance of herself in my sleepy visage and realized my question was a common refrain as I was growing up and looking for something of myself in my adoptive parents.

The nurse had stood up from her station and joined me unnoticed, and so I was startled when she asked, "Would you like to hold him?"

I didn't know what to say at first. Up until then, Adrienne was the only one of us to take him in her arms and sustain him in those fleeting moments when his hunger came calling. Again I thought of my birth mother holding me for the first and last time.

"Here," the nurse said. "Sit down." She pulled a chair over to me. "And take off your shirt." I looked at her. "Babies like being skin to skin," she said.

Who doesn't? I thought.

I took off my shirt and sat down. She retrieved my son, who twitched a little at this new disturbance but never opened his eyes. I took all of him into my arms, his head resting on my chest, his diapered butt supported by my right forearm, and felt his back expand and contract with ease.

"How does that feel?" the nurse asked.

Like relief, I wanted to say, but I was overcome by another sensation: how warm he felt, like fever made flesh, and how it spread throughout me until we were two bodies incandescing as one in that pale yellow light. I looked at the nurse, suddenly incapable of speech. Eventually, she walked over and took Simon from me. I finally exhaled. I hadn't realized I had been holding my breath.

Holding my breath around Simon turned out to be a necessity. Our first attempt at a family vacation was in 2009, not long before Simon turned three. We were with my sister and her family. A day after our arrival in northern Wisconsin, we left after Simon vomited all over himself, the car seat, and Adrienne's cleavage. With no washing machine in the house and no laundromat within fifty miles, we had no choice but to depart early. Our second attempt, a year later and again with my sister, abruptly ended when Simon reversed gears and shot copious amounts of diarrhea out his bottom and all over the rental cabin living room. Despite this, the invitation was again extended (we were, after all, family). So we packed up Adrienne's Ford Focus that mid-July 2011 and left Eau Claire—the city where I'd grown up, gone to college, met my wife, and had for many years made a quietly contented life—for a long weekend in Minocqua, Wisconsin. We kept our fingers crossed that, this time, we'd last more than a day.

We were running late. I called my brother-in-law, Jim, and told him we'd be there around dinnertime.

"When you get here," he said, "you'll see two buildings. There's the cabin and then more lodging directly across from it." He paused. "You guys can have that space all to yourselves."

"Exile for past offenses?" I asked.

He laughed. "It's pretty crowded in the main cabin. We figured you'd appreciate the room." He paused again. "I'm actually kind of jealous."

"Uh-huh," I said.

I adjusted the rearview mirror to see Simon in the back seat. He was almost five years old, belted in his car seat, the thick straps crisscrossing a gray T-shirt and locking between red shorts. His window was down, his blond hair wispy, disheveled, and standing on end as though someone had rubbed an inflated balloon against his head. He directed his gaze at the towering cornstalks whooshing by the window. "What're you thinking about, buddy?" I asked, breaking his trance.

His brown eyes fluttered before finding their perch on the duffel bag beside him. "About what's in this." He patted the nylon fabric. "When I can take it out."

I glanced at Adrienne. She whispered, "At least it's not the dress." *But why couldn't it have been the Barbie doll*, I thought as I watched the roadside markers tick by in their blurry retreat, like beings in possession of our most precious secret in a mad dash to tell the world.

We pulled off the paved road and slowly followed a rocky trail through thickening greenery onto the property. A monarch butterfly vectored off the hood, and fecund vegetation scraped both sides of the car. A leafy branch swiped at Simon through his open window. This was a world of biological impulse, the wild desire to grow, to live, regardless of any human imposition.

The main cabin came into view: a brown two-story, abundantly windowed, and a screened-in porch out front. This was where my sister, brother-in-law, and their kids would be lodging. Like Jim said, there was a second building to our left, much smaller and porchless, where Adrienne, Simon, and I would be sleeping. The word *exile* popped into my head again like a comic-strip thought bubble. I didn't blame them.

I switched off the ignition, and Simon bounded from the car. In the time it took me to meander to a halt, he had unstrapped himself from his car seat, zipped open the duffel bag, and quietly slipped his arms through the white elastic bands on a pair of gold-tinged fairy wings. From a distance, it might pass for an oversized and loosely tethered backpack. In the few feet between our car and the porch where my family had massed to greet us, the wings were unmistakable.

"Can't you wait until we see everyone and get settled?" I asked.

"Nope," he said.

I heard Jim call from the top of the steps. Tall and slender, he stood in a T-shirt and shorts, beer can in hand. My sister, Nikki, was next to him, eyes hidden behind a pair of brown sunglasses. On the remaining stairs, and arranged in descending order, from oldest to youngest, were their three children: Caleb, Campbell, and Jett, all shirtless despite the day's autumn-like chill.

Simon stood now stationary at the foot of the porch steps, grinning widely at his family. Adrienne and I grabbed our bags, slammed the car doors, and shuffled to his side. It was like intruding upon some staring contest. I thought about the butterfly effect, revising it in my head: a fairy flaps its wings, and an entire family goes silent at a remote cabin in Wisconsin. Simon was more wings than boy. Finally, one of his cousins spoke: "Cool wings." Simon, buoyed by this apparent approbation, ascended the steps, and life resumed its regular rhythms of small talk and good cheer:

"How was the drive?" Nikki asked.

"Why don't you toss your things in your cabin and join us for dinner?" Jim said.

A green snake curved across our path and into the nearest undergrowth. Adrienne and I carried our things into our cabin. The screen door banged loudly behind us. There was a comfortable-looking couch, a table and chairs in the kitchen, and three bedrooms down a shadowy wood-paneled hallway.

"Not bad," Adrienne said.

"Hardly feels like exile at all," I said. I snapped the lights on and off, ran the faucet, and opened the door of the empty refrigerator. "I wonder how Simon's doing."

"He's fine," Adrienne said. "We're with family."

We joined Jim and Nikki on the porch. Large red and green coolers doubled as mini-tables for the kids to allow the adults room at the big table hefted out from the kitchen. A picnic table to the left of the cabin overlooked the shoreline, and a white dock with chipping paint was spotted with white and green goose shit. Then, finally, the cool expanse of the lake.

"Pretty, huh?" Nikki said, setting down our plates, sunglasses atop her head.

Winged Simon sprinted by. We both watched him. "It's amazing how much energy they have at that age," my sister said. She turned toward me. "How's everything going?" she asked.

"Fine," I said. I called Simon over for dinner.

"How are Mom and Dad?" she asked, changing the subject.

"Mom's doing well," I said. "Dad's as goofy as ever." She smiled. Nikki was adopted, too. Although we had some epic clashes as kids, and sometimes as adults, we also took refuge in this special bond we shared.

Adrienne opened a wine bottle.

"That's my cue," Nikki said. "Come on, brother." She grabbed me by the arm and pulled me to the table.

Jim helped the kids serve themselves spaghetti, getting flecks of sauce on his hands and arms. He talked with Simon about the trip, the wings comically glaring.

After dinner the kids ducked back outside to play. The grown-ups felt the shoulder grip of our distant city-worlds relax in the early evening light. Adrienne and Nikki talked at the table while Jim cleared our plates. I moved to sit on one of the coolers. Jim soon joined me, opening the adjacent cooler, fishing out a beer, and sitting next to me.

"Simon grew some wings since last we saw him," Jim said, cracking open his can.

I scooted back on the cooler and leaned against the porch screen's wooden frame. "He's evolving into a very interesting person."

"Well, whoever he is," Jim said, sipping his beer, "I think he's cool."

I wanted to hug him for this, for the unqualified kindness he'd shown Simon since we arrived. He simply saw Simon as his nephew, not a boy who preferred to wear fairy wings or play with Barbies. The moment was interrupted when his youngest, Jett, barreled through the porch door in search of refreshment. I was seated atop the "kiddie" cooler and quickly stood up so he could remove a root beer. "Hey, Dad," he said. "Can we hit up the go-kart track in town tomorrow?"

"We'll talk about it later, Jett," Jim said. "I'm talking with Andy right now."

"Okay." Jett exited the porch as quickly as he'd entered, and I was simultaneously seized with an image of my sister and her husband fretting over what to name this third child and impressed with their prescience.

All parents experience a kind of dumbstruck wonder when it comes to their kids. You never know what you're going to get. But usually we think of that "not knowing" in terms of our kids being athletic or musical, not that our baby boys will see themselves as girls and women. An interest in Barbie dolls was the first clue Simon was atypical compared to boys his age. Other clues followed. For example, I often referred to Simon as my little Lon Chaney after the silent movie era star famous for his special makeup transformations in roles like *The Phantom of the*

Opera and *The Hunchback of Notre Dame* and which earned him the title "Man of a Thousand Faces." It was also a subtle way of connecting Simon to one of my own affinities: the horror film. In his playroom was a storage bin full of costumes salvaged from department store post-Halloween markdowns. There was an alien, a mummy, a vampire, and, my personal favorite, a swamp creature, the same variety that had successfully kept me on the shoreline for years as a kid. He would rotate through each and role-play with Adrienne and me, growling and giving chase while we shrieked and ran and feigned terror. The costume bin was soon overflowing.

However, his identification was now with the female characters in otherwise boy-centered stories (Hermione in *Harry Potter* and Annabeth in *Percy Jackson*). Gradually, newer acquisitions began to replace the masculine monsters of old. First, there was a green Medusa skull cap sprouting plush snakes, followed by a black witch's hat, transitory pieces that opened the door to a Hannah Montana wig and, finally, Simon's personal favorite, a dress. Nothing fancy. It was simple, blue, falling just below his knees, and it fit like neither he nor the dress were ever strangers. As parents, we'd long resisted fettering his play to gender norms, but the dress hit differently. A boy in a dress felt like a statement. It would draw attention to him, for good or ill, more so than a Barbie doll or even a pair of fairy wings. And so the dress was something he could wear in the privacy of his home as opposed to out in the open with its unpredictable public.

When it came to my sister's kids, all three—not just Jett—had an unrestrained enthusiasm for their father's passion. Jim drove race cars in the summer as part of the Sports Car Club of America (SCCA). People from across the country traveled to different road courses to compete, and the Road America course was one hour from their home in Appleton, Wisconsin. It frequently came up in their casual conversations. It was nearly impossible not to stumble over *Cars* movie merchandise when the kids were around. Meanwhile, I struggled to see any of myself in Simon and wondered if there was anything of himself he could possibly see in me.

It wasn't so different from the situation with my own father. My dad worked in data processing before he retired; a life spent in numbers always carried, for me at least, a masculine connotation of logic detached from emotion. I, on the other hand, was a high school English teacher. Once, a colleague paraphrased a student's assessment of the kind of person who'd take a job like mine as "a bit light in the loafers." While I was growing up, my father took pride in an immaculate lawn. Now, there was visible discomfort on his face, in his body language, whenever he visited our home and what I jokingly referred to as my "receding lawn line." Some of this alienation, especially when I was younger, was attributable to the fact I was adopted. I was biologically different from my father. And it was easy to hold this against him or to blame myself for not measuring up. But we also had things in common. For example, my dad and I both enjoyed playing poker together one Friday a month. What did I have in common with Simon?

I could hear Adrienne's voice in my head: *He's only four*. Then, suddenly, out loud, "Hey, Andy. You promised me a beer and a view of the sunset."

I looked up to see the porch door close behind her.

"I did?"

"Enjoy, you two," Jim said, heading for the kitchen.

I grabbed two bottles of porter from the cooler and went to sit alongside my wife at the picnic table. The sun had yet to set over a line of pine trees beyond the edge of Plummer Lake. The last of the day's boaters were out floating, their conversation drifting to us without form, like the lapping water, their laughter our only clue as to where one thought ended for another to begin. Neighbors brought wood to their fire pit. There was a lonely call from a loon. Insect sounds. My sister turned on the porch light in anticipation of the night and then the stars so bright one might look up and believe in the practicality of wishing. But it was still too early for the fireflies. Not quite dark enough for the mosquitoes to rise from their dampened bowers and come biting. It was a purplish, half-lit country, and it felt magical, as if forces beyond our purview had silently replaced our world with their own while we drank and talked. Into that changeling light came Simon, his wings vibrating in the wind his rushing body made and his feet leaving small impressions in the grass.

Nikki came out of the cabin with an armful of marshmallows, chocolate bars, and graham crackers and shouted, "S'mores!"

"On it," said Jim, charging out of the porch and down to the fire pit.

Simon circled us and the picnic table and then veered off toward his cousins, who were searching the bramble for the perfect skewer. I silently hoped he might relax on the wings and join the other boys in the leaves and the dirt.

"We'll have to check him for ticks," Adrienne said.

I inhaled deeply. "I could get used to this."

She elbowed me in the ribs. "You are used to this, teacher man." A jab at my summers off. Meanwhile, Adrienne worked year-round in social services.

I gestured behind me. "I mean the seclusion. Nature. Reminds me of when I was a Cub Scout."

"Yeah?" she asked. "And how long did that last?"

"I don't know." I raised my right hand and started counting. "One ... two ... maybe three badges?"

"Can you tie a knot?" she asked.

I held up my feet. "Do shoelaces count?"

"Those are sandals."

"Exactly."

Adrienne grinned. "I bet you didn't even go to camp as a kid."

I was too much of a homebody to be bothered with archery, boating, and bugs. Not much had changed, really. I lived in the town where I grew up. I taught at the high school I graduated from eighteen years ago. I still watched the same cheesy horror movies I did as a kid.

"Well," I said. "There was Camp Crystal Lake."

She rolled her eyes. "God, not those awful slasher movies."

"And then there was *Sleepaway Camp*. Remember that one?" I asked.

"Shhh," she cut me off. We were back on Simon's flight path. "How was the s'more, honey?"

Simon answered with a sound not unlike the night wind. He swooped in at us—the great moth-child.

"Hey, buddy." I plucked him from the air and held him close for a moment, smelling woodsmoke in his hair. "Did you save your mom and me any?"

"Maybe," he smiled.

"Maybe?" I tickled him. "Maybe you better get your butt back there and make me one."

"Dad, watch the wings."

"Oops," I said. "Sorry." I loosened my hold without letting go.

"Are you getting cold?" Adrienne asked. "Do you need your sweatshirt?"

Looking around, I could see we were the only ones who hadn't yet changed out of our T-shirts, shorts, and sandals.

"I'm fine," Simon said, twisting a bit in my arms, his lean stomach slipping out from under his shirt.

"Well, I'm not," Adrienne said, standing up from the picnic

table. "I'm gonna go grab mine. Do you want yours, Andy?"

"Sure," I said. "I imagine we'll make a fine feast with all this exposed flesh."

I imitated the sound of a whining insect homing in on Simon, who pulled himself free of my grasp and took once again to the air.

"You'll never catch me, Dad," Simon said. "My wings are too fast."

"Touché," I said. "And I'm too old."

"Too drunk," Adrienne whispered.

"Definitely not that ... yet," I said.

"Where does this trail go?" Simon had finally noticed the pathway to the lake.

"Down to the water," Adrienne said.

"Can I check it out?" Simon asked.

Adrienne looked at me. I looked at the sky. The last light drew down soft as breath over the tree line. "There's your sunset," I said.

"Stay away from the water," Adrienne called.

"Okay," Simon said, already halfway down the trail.

Simon reached the bottom and, true to his word, avoided the water's edge. Instead, he stayed to the left of the dock and skirted the neighbors' property. Their fire pit crackled and heaved up its orange and yellow light. Three men ringed round it, slouching in lawn chairs and clutching beers in their bear claw hands resting easily on their bellies. I imagined hairy arms burned by outdoor labor beneath an unforgiving sun, perhaps a faded, birthmark blue tattoo. I watched as they looked up in unison to behold our moth-child drawn to their fire.

One man turned to his friends and said, "Fellas, I think the fairies are out tonight."

A chorus of chuckles.

Another said, "Son, take those girlie things off and just toss them right here on the fire."

I felt my hands clenching. I stood up and took two steps toward the path. A sobering thought interceded: *Three of them, one of you. And three times the alcohol. You know how this movie ends.* I called out to Simon instead, but it was the attention and unwanted derision from adults who should know better but often don't that drove him back up the trail toward our picnic table.

"How is he?" Adrienne asked, sitting down next to me and handing me my sweatshirt. She hadn't heard the men's comments.

"You can ask him," I said. My hands were still shaking. "Here he comes."

Simon blew past us, his arms slipping from the elastic bands that hugged those gold wings to his body. They lay crumpled at our feet. We watched as he ignored his cousin Jett's call and tromped into our cabin, the door squeaking into place behind him.

"What was that about?" Adrienne asked.

"I overheard those guys down there make a comment about the wings," I said. Rather than condemn the men I could not confront, I blamed my four-year-old son. "I knew we shouldn't have let him bring them along."

"Oh, come on," Adrienne said. "It was a compromise. Remember?"

I thought of the dress in a storage bin in his playroom. "I remember."

"I'm sure he'll be fine once he cools off," Adrienne said.

"Will he?"

"Sure," Adrienne said.

"What if it isn't just the wings, Adrienne?"

"What do you mean?" she asked, bending to retrieve them from the ground.

"I mean," I said, looking back down the path, "I just worry is all."

The sun was up early the following day; the heat came later. By then the lake was an irresistible draw. After lunch we all changed into our bathing suits and maneuvered down the trail, towels slung over shoulders. Jim and I brought up the rear, carrying a cooler between us. Adrienne held Simon's hand as they slid their way to the bottom. I glimpsed the shit-spattered dock. No geese in sight, but they'd left quite a calling card hardening in the midday sun. I made a mental note to find something to scrape it off with later. My nephews were splashing in the shallow water, eyes scanning and fingers sifting for vacant mollusk shells in the detrital wash along the shoreline. Simon had left his wings at the foot of his bed where Adrienne had deposited them the night before. I watched him slump into a soft patch of sand and pick at the sparse growth surrounding him, tossing the green blades into the lake. Jett called to him, "Come in, Simon." Simon looked up for a moment and returned to his uprooting.

"What do you think?" Adrienne asked.

"I think he's still upset about those guys laughing at him last night," I said.

"I get it," she said. "But the kid has to be able to move on."

"Let me talk to him."

I left Adrienne with my sister and brother-in-law, their toes moving beneath the warm sand. Jim opened the cooler, pulling two beers from the ice. "Got one waiting for you, Andy," he said. I waved at him and then sat down next to Simon, who did not acknowledge me. I searched for a polished stone suitable for skipping.

"You doing okay, buddy?" I asked.

He continued to pick at the long grass.

"I mean, water, this is your thing," I said. Although motivating him to engage in physical activity was often difficult, we couldn't pull him out of pools, lakes, the bathtub. Adrienne and I had dubbed him the "water creature."

"I'm just not feeling it right now." His voice sounded oddly adult. I figured he'd picked up the phrase from Adrienne or me when we were trying to decide on a restaurant or movie.

"Is this because of those men and your wings?" I asked.

Simon stiffened, directing his eyes toward their cold fire pit, vacant lawn chairs, and empty cans strewn in the dirt. "I don't really want to talk about that."

I skimmed a rock three hops over the lake's still surface. "You know, I think your cousins would appreciate you swimming with them," I said. "Looks like they're having fun."

"How would you know?" he said. "You never go swimming with me."

Unlike Simon, I greatly disliked swimming, especially in bodies of water whose bottoms were obscured and creatures two to three times my length were lurking. Too many lake monster horror movies as a kid, maybe. I remember knee boarding in high school, toppling over not long after that first great acceleration, bobbing in my life vest, waiting for my best friend, Chad, to bring the boat back around while other friends shouted from the shore, "Sturgeon! Watch out for the sturgeon!"

I looked at Simon and said, "This is true."

"Why, though?" he asked. "Don't you want to swim with me?"

"It's not that I don't want to swim with you." I cast my eyes over the water. Thought I saw a fish jump. Radiating ripples the only evidence. "I just get ... nervous, that's all."

"Why nervous?" he asked.

I thought for a moment. "You know how you don't like your closet door to be open in the night?" Simon nodded. "It's like that," I said. "I don't like all that unknown beneath me."

"But you and Mom always tell me I shouldn't be afraid of the unknown," he said. "That I should face what I'm afraid of."

He had me on the ropes. I thought of my dad attempting to build bridges with me as a kid. "Tell you what," I said, standing up and shaking the sand off my hands. I pointed at the dock. "I will execute the greatest human cannonball this side of the circus if you agree to join your cousins for a swim."

Simon looked from his cousins to his sandy feet and nodded. "Okay," he said.

"Excellent."

I let the towel slide from my shoulders and side-winked at Adrienne, who was watching alongside my sister and brother-in-law. I emptied my lungs and ran to the dock, hopping up onto the wooden platform and then bobbling a bit as I attempted to avoid stepping in the minefield of goose shit, tiny green piles of it dispersed haphazardly along my pathway until my feet found the edge and I jumped, pulling my knees to my chest and holding my breath (once again, for Simon), hearing my nephews shout, "Yeah!" and then dropping into the unknown. The splash came muffled to my ears. The pressure was immediate. The cold shock forced my eyes and lips open, and for a moment I saw the sun cutting shafts of light through all that murky green. I wondered how much of its color was due to goose droppings in the water, and then I was up like a submersible suddenly rising from the seafloor. I swam to where he was sitting on the shore and lumbered out, my trunks ballooning with lake water, a tangle of weeds around my ankles. "How was that?" I asked.

Simon giggled. "Better than a belly flop."

I made a move for him. "You better get in there before I show you a belly flop."

He squealed away from me and was soon frolicking with his cousins.

We've done it, I thought, peering out at my happy family. We made it through a full day of vacation without banishment.

Two weeks later, on a Thursday, back at home, I awoke in terrible discomfort, wracked with abdominal pain, which soon gave way to blustering, embarrassing gas. I spent much of my day near a toilet, wishing for privacy, though I often heard Adrienne stifling her laughter beyond the bathroom door. Later that evening, believing I was on the mend, I invited several close colleagues over for food and movies. My friend and department chair, Dave, descended the stairs to the basement, the rest of us in tow.

"Have you been dropping ass down here or what?" he asked.

I felt my face flush and considered my response. "Maybe …" I said, filling bowls with chips and glasses with ice.

Thirty minutes into the first movie, I felt my guts swell and churn. Not wanting to befoul the basement commode, I tried to slink off to the facilities two floors above. I shut the door, sat down, and braced for propulsive fury. When I stood to flush, I saw the toilet bowl filled with blood. I wasn't yet in pain. I opened the door and called for Adrienne. Soon she was standing next to me. "That's not good," she said.

"Maybe it's just a one-time freak occurrence."

"Maybe it's something more," she said. "I think we need to go to the hospital, Andy. Seriously."

"I'll keep an eye on it," I said, flushing the toilet and heading back down the stairs, her eyes following until I disappeared around the corner.

Within the next half hour, I had two more bloody bowel movements. By now my friends had noticed my frequent coming and going and asked if I was okay. I gave in and confessed that my stomach was *en fuego*. There was some snickering. "That explains the smell," Dave said. One of my friends suggested it might be hemorrhoids. He even called a doctor friend of his in New York, who quickly diagnosed my symptoms over the phone and recommended I lie in a warm bath. "Sit down, Andy," Dave said. "You're gonna be fine."

Fifteen minutes later I excused myself yet again. I remember climbing the two flights of stairs and crumpling midway. I was dizzy, weak. I called for Adrienne. She gasped at the sight of me prostrate on the staircase. She held her hands to her mouth. Instead of crying, she helped me to the toilet. "You're going to the hospital," she demanded. "Right now."

"What about Simon?"

"He's down the street," she said. "I'll call over there and let them know what's going on."

I thought of Simon in his fairy wings, floating, angelic, in the firelight beside the lake. My fragile boy. My heart. "Make sure they don't tell him any details," I told Adrienne. "I don't want to scare him."

Adrienne draped my arm over her shoulder and wrapped her other arm around my waist. She eased me down the stairs. She told my friends they were welcome to stay and finish the movie, but she was driving me to the emergency room. My friends emerged from the basement, concerned and contrite. Dave's eyes widened at the pale sight of me, his expression blank, at a loss for words.

The cramping and expulsing continued throughout my preliminary exam in the ER, and I was soon admitted for a hospital stay. Adrienne stood at my bedside. "I don't want to leave you here like this."

"It's okay," I said. "I'm already feeling better." She frowned at me and my lie. "It's late, and you should probably rescue our neighbors from Simon. I'll be alright."

Adrienne bent down and kissed me on my forehead. "I'll be back first thing in the morning," she said.

My stomach calmed for the moment, so I closed my eyes to try and get some sleep. As I grew drowsy in my hospital room, the amber glow from the parking lot stretched across my ceiling. Simon wasn't even five—more baby than boy but also not a boy at all. He played with Barbies. He flitted in the summer light in fairy wings. He preferred a dress to his other clothes. Only in this liminal dream state could I admit what these facts were adding up to, the truth about him. In the morning, a hazy summer Friday, I returned to my former self, the part of me that believed that his girlish ways were only a phase. Like the blood moving through my troubled bowels, whatever was occurring in my son would surely, eventually, pass.

The gastroenterologist was a serious-looking man, clean-shaven, with well-coiffed hair. He asked if I had a family history of ulcers or colitis. I shrugged. "I'm adopted," I said. "I don't know much about my family medical history."

All I knew was that I was born in rural western Wisconsin to a fifteen-year-old girl. My biological father was just seventeen years old and not around much after the pregnancy. I had long wondered about them, especially her—whether my quirks came from either birth parent. My hair, my need for glasses, my penchant for reading books over engaging with sports. Now I wondered about their guts, too.

The gastroenterologist frowned. "I see," he said and told me he'd scheduled me for a colonoscopy in a few hours. I'd have to chug two liters of liquid laxative in ninety minutes. I vowed to dig deeper into my medical history.

When Adrienne arrived, after leaving Simon with my parents, she found me in my hospital bed, two pillows propped behind me, a few cups into my drinking game. "It helps to think of them as shots," I said and downed another. I gagged. "Tastes about as good as Jägermeister."

Adrienne set her purse on the counter and came over to kiss me.

"How's Simon doing?" I asked.

"Worried," she said. "I told him your tummy wasn't feeling the best, but you were being taken care of and should be fine in no time."

"Did that help him?" I asked, but I had to hurry to the bathroom before she could answer. I wasn't allowed to flush. The nursing assistant collected my stool and took it away for interpretation by the doctors. I stared into the commode at all that blood and said, "I thought I came here to stop doing this."

There was a knock at the door. A nurse entered and helped me onto a gurney. She wheeled me to my destination while Adrienne walked by my side. The doctor I'd met earlier that morning sensed my nervousness. "The drugs will help you feel better," he said. I was helped off the gurney and onto an examination table. Adrienne touched my shoulder and went out to the waiting area. A monitor allowed me to follow the camera as it snaked through my guts. *How nice*, I thought. Then the drugs took effect, and I thought no more.

Two hours later I was back in my room, coming to my senses. Adrienne was with me. There was another knock—an endless parade of knocks—and the doctor came into view at the foot of my bed. The colonoscopy had revealed an open wound along my digestive tract, which they were able to cauterize. "An anomaly," he said, "not linked to any other agent. Everything looks pretty clean in there."

It ought to, I thought.

"Well, that's good news," Adrienne said. She stood up. "I'm gonna go pick up Simon. I'll be back later." She grabbed her purse, crossed the room, and looked back. "Let me know if you need anything from home."

I thought of my dreams of Simon. "Tell my little Lon Chaney I love him."

I expected the blood to stop now that the doctor had identified the cause. Still, throughout the day I continued to fill the toilet with my bloody stool, and the young female CNAs continued to take it away. It was mortifying. I knew there was a smell even if I'd become inured to it. I remember hearing one girl say to another when they assumed I was out of earshot, "Whew! You always know when there's a GI bleed on the floor." Doubly mortifying was confronting a CNA I knew from my creative writing class several years earlier. *Fourth period*, I thought. *Middle row. Three desks from the front.* She had written a poem about her grandmother caught out in a storm as a child and tied that to her grandmother's struggle with lung cancer. The imagery of that poem was indelible enough to show up unbidden in this moment. I had been teaching high school juniors and seniors for thirteen years. When I saw the nurse assistant last, she was crossing the stage for her diploma in an overcrowded, overheated gymnasium, the future incessantly flapping in the folds of her graduation gown. The polar blue of that garment traded in for the traditional blue of her hospital scrubs.

"Mr. Patrie," she said. "It's been a while."

"Andy," I said. I imagined her texting her friends from her high school class: *Guess whose ass I had to wipe today?* "How are you?"

"Living the dream," she grinned. "I'd ask how you're doing, but I guess you've had better days than this."

She got right to work. I could hear her swapping out one receptacle for another, tidying up after me, all the while talking about herself, her younger brother, who she wondered if I remembered—anything other than the smell. I wanted to respond to her, to ask about that grandmother, but all I did was sit there in my bed in anticipation of yet another humiliating reaction to my unsettled bowels. I thought again, for the thousandth time, of Simon, wingless on the shoreline, still stewing on those men who had laughed at him, and I shrank further into the thin, white fabric of my hospital gown. When she finally finished, told me it was nice seeing me, and closed the door behind her, I felt my dimming frame alight in her kindness.

The internist came to see me on Saturday. He was in his mid-forties, with a slight belly pushing against his button-up shirt and jeans, a stethoscope around his neck. He said I could start eating solid foods again. I asked if I could go home. "Not today," he said.

"But I thought it was only an anomaly?" I asked.

"I'll just feel more comfortable after the results come back from your stool samples," he said.

I sighed, reclined in my bed, and looked out the window at all the other windows on the face of the building across from me. I thought I saw someone briefly appear at one of them, an IV stand pulled up beside them, the top of which arched like a reaper's blade over the patient's head. I wondered what the doctors would find hiding in my blood.

CLUMSY LOVE

Adrienne came to visit in the early evening. My parents had volunteered to take Simon out for a burger and then back to their place. My dinner had just arrived. I ordered the salmon. I figured the fishy smell wouldn't bother anybody, given the circumstances.

"You know, Simon would like to come see you," Adrienne said, sitting down in the chair next to me.

"I'd say he's in luck," I said, checking an invisible calendar. "I'm wide open tomorrow."

"How're you holding up?"

I sipped some water. "I really want to go home."

She watched me eat. I was hunched over the portable table drawn across my bed.

"At least there's Shark Week," I said, motioning to the television mounted to the wall across from me.

If I closed my eyes, I could imagine Adrienne and me out to dinner at Houligans, cozied up in a booth suffused in muted lamplight, our conversation twining us together. But my eyes were open, and I felt my stomach drop as if I'd accidentally nudged a wine glass from the table and sent it crashing to the floor.

Adrienne saw my face. "What's wrong?"

I pressed a hand to my abdomen. "Something's definitely not right."

The cramping had returned. I got up to use the bathroom. It was a copious amount of blood, even by my standards, and it refused to cease. "You'd better get a nurse," I grunted.

Adrienne pressed the button alerting the nurses' station. Two of them came in. "This feels different," I said.

By the time the nurses got me back into bed, I could feel the urge to go again. A nurse instructed me to raise my rump, and then she slid a bedpan under me. I filled it in seconds. I lifted my hips, and the nurse exchanged it for another. I remember feeling the cold metal against my thighs and then more cramping and the bleeding like some biblical reckoning. How much blood could a person lose?

After I'd filled the second bedpan, a third was slid into position, and someone called for more help. I remember the room suddenly crowding with people, Adrienne hovering in the background, her eyes brimming with tears, and the machine monitoring my vital signs erratically beeping. A nurse was saying, "Tip him on his head," and I felt the bed tilting. *No, I've got a bedpan full of my blood underneath me*, I thought, and then my vision started pixelating, and I lost my hearing. The scab from Friday's cauterization had sloughed off before its time. The artery it was covering quickly began to bleed out. Later, Adrienne told me I turned ashen. The nurse had the presence of mind to tilt the bed until my feet were in the air and my head was near the ground, diverting the blood flow to my brain and saving my life. Now, with the hemorrhaging contained and the bed righted, I was moved to the Intensive Care Unit, where I would receive several blood transfusions over the next couple of days. If the scab didn't hold this time, I'd need to undergo surgery for an ostomy. For the first time, I was afraid that I could die. I thought of Simon. There was a gathering storm on the horizon, even if I couldn't bring myself to name it yet, and he would need me around. I had to get better. Thankfully, the new scab held, and I was transferred out of the ICU.

A few days later, the internist came to see me, looking as freshly scrubbed and casual as before. "We finally have the results back from your stool samples," he said. "The cause of all your distress."

"Okay," I said.

"This guy," he said, holding up a photo printed from a

computer. I sat up in my bed and leaned closer. It looked like several dozen worms suddenly shocked from the earth and clumped together for safety. "*Campylobacter.* A kind of bacteria that lives in various fowl."

I grasped the photo from his hand. "How?"

"Typically, people get it from eating undercooked poultry," he said. He explained symptoms, like the abdominal pain I experienced the night I came into the ER, show up about two weeks after first contact. It takes a while for enough of the bacteria to build up. He took the photo from me. "What were you doing two weeks prior to your symptoms?"

I thought back. "Staying at a cabin," I said. "Minocqua."

"You eat any chicken there?"

"No," I said. "Mostly burgers, brats, that kind of thing."

He told me our immune systems can usually handle something like *Campylobacter* but that it could do the kind of damage sustained by my digestive tract.

"So," I asked, "it wasn't an anomaly?"

"No. Given the presence and sheer amount of *Campylobacter* in your stool, I'm afraid I have to disagree with my colleague's initial diagnosis."

I looked down at my stomach.

"Are you sure you can't remember eating any chicken?" he asked. "It's important because we may have to follow up with the manufacturer."

"No, I'm sorry. I—" I stopped. I thought of the dock, slicked with goose shit. "You said this thing lives inside of various fowl, right?"

"That's right."

"Like, waterfowl, too?"

"Sure," he said. "Ducks, geese …"

"Geese."

"What about geese?" he asked.

"There was this dock," I said, "on the lake where we stayed. It was covered in goose poop. I mean just covered. I jumped off it one afternoon to cheer up my son." I shook my head. "I must've gotten some of it in my mouth."

"Could be."

"I wasn't the only one in the water that day. But I'm the only one who got sick."

"Lucky you," he said.

I nodded. "At least it isn't cancer, eh?"

I was put on an aggressive five-day antibiotic. I was also warned about weakness as my body took its time to rebuild the iron in my blood. It would not be uncommon for me to feel dizzy or winded when climbing stairs.

Later that day Adrienne and Simon came to pick me up. I remember the way he brightened at the sight of me, the way his shoes squeaked as he ran across the floor, and the fluid motion of those gold fairy wings behind him, closing then opening like hands in applause or prayer or both. I raised my torso and swung my legs over the side of the bed to receive him. He hit me with a hug, and I cleaved to his body as if it had been more than a week we'd been apart, wondering what changes nature might have wrought in my absence. Adrienne watched the reunion from the doorway.

"Is it true, Dad?" Simon asked, removing his chin from my neck and looking me in the eyes.

"Is what true?"

"You ate bird poop?" He was trying not to smile.

I looked at Adrienne. She shrugged.

"It's true," I said. "Not intentionally, of course ..."

He interrupted, "Just like me." He relinquished his embrace and capered about the room. "I not intentionally ate poop, too."

Simon was well aware of the story of his first meconium-filled breath following Adrienne's C-section and, like most four-year-olds, obsessed with all things scatological.

Adrienne shushed Simon and then glanced down the hall to make sure no one had heard him.

"It's an exclusive club," I said.

A CNA brought a wheelchair into the room for me and helped me into it. Adrienne got behind me and gripped the handles, leaning down to whisper in my ear, "Next time you want to bond with your kid, try playing Barbies instead." We followed Simon to the elevator, which took us to the ground floor.

The door dinged open, and Simon took off ahead of us. I watched him glide past waiting areas, watched those wings draw the inevitable attention of those who had lost interest in reading the latest in celebrity gossip or whatever was playing on daytime television. I remembered our conversation about facing fears before I leapt into the lake, and as my wheelchair trundled along, I thought about how sometimes our fears still find a way to win, how something so small, bacteria or a careless comment, can upend our lives. And I tried to read in those staring faces which ones most resembled those jeering men around the fire pit, which ones he might have to one day confront, which ones, it seemed, couldn't help but try and clip those wings. When he got to the revolving door, stopping before it could spin him out into the parking lot, he momentarily vanished in the flood of afternoon light beyond it. I imagined membranous wings pumping him aloft until some wind current took hold, and he could safely drift above our world and all its judging eyes.

THE KINDNESS OF STRANGERS

The grass was yellow and withered, crisp under bare feet. Sprinklers shot plumes of water high into the air in front yards up and down the block. Plastic kiddie pools sat unattended in the noonday sun. Fickle breezes pushed inflatable toys across the surfaces pocked with stray grass blades and black bugs. Somewhere a dog was barking. It was an August afternoon. We hadn't had rain in weeks. I came outside to edge my lawn. I'd spent the weeks since I'd returned from the hospital cooped up inside, watching television and waiting for my abdomen to heal. My retired father was given to unannounced visits, and it was not uncommon to look outside and find him tending to my yard. Finally feeling better, I figured I'd be proactive for a change and forestall him.

Adrienne was at work. Simon sat on our front steps. He brought two plastic buckets out with him: one filled with chalk for drawing and writing rudimentary phrases and one with Barbie dolls. He sat on the top step, gripped one of the dolls close to his chest, and began drawing a butterfly with a piece of blue chalk.

I went to the shed in the backyard and returned with a shovel. Simon was shading in the butterfly's wings. "Nice drawing, buddy," I said as I walked by. I received no reply. I wasn't long into my work when I paused to run my shirtsleeve across my forehead. I saw a man walking toward me out of the corner of my eye. He was wearing a black polo shirt, olive-colored shorts, and sandals. He had thick dark hair and glasses. I could see stubble beginning to form along his cheeks and chin. "I'm Ari," he said. His accent was South Asian, possibly Indian.

"Andy," I said.

"I'm the new neighbor," he said, gesturing to the white two-story to the right of our home.

"Welcome to the neighborhood."

We shook hands.

I could feel him looking at Simon on the steps, now playing with his dolls, and I shifted my body slightly to shield him from view. "That's Simon," I said. "My son."

"I have a daughter, Gita, about Simon's age. She's with my partner, Rachel, at the moment."

I looked over at the solitary compact car parked in their driveway free of any signs of a family in transition. "You pack light," I said.

He followed my eyes and chuckled. "We're not moving in for a couple weeks," he said. "I'm here to pick up the keys. I saw you and thought I'd introduce myself."

"I appreciate that," I said.

"Anyway, I'll leave you to your edging. Seems a bit too industrious on a bloody hot day like this."

If nothing else, he was disarming.

"Be seeing you," he said and returned to his car.

I stuck the shovel into the ground, crunched down with my foot, and scraped away another loose chunk of soil.

It didn't take long for Gita and Simon to find each other. It may have been a glimpse of Simon on the sidewalk through her front window. Or a blurred sighting of Gita on her steps in our haste between house and car. Their proximity preordained a friendship. While Simon got along with the neighbor boys and his cousins, Jett, Campbell, and Caleb, it was also easy for him to detach and run solo. With Gita, things were different. They were inseparable. And their togetherness also meant more contact between the parents.

One fall evening, as I finished mowing the lawn, thinking how it would never be a golf course green like my father's, I looked over to see Ari standing by the picket fence that ran along part of the property line between our homes. His right forearm nestled between two posts, his hand clutching a bottle of beer, his left holding another. An anthropology professor at the local university, Ari didn't strike me as a double-fister, even if he was in academia.

It was going on six o'clock, and though the sun had swung to the west, the light was still everywhere, especially in the trees, one of which Simon and Gita claimed as their own: a sturdy elm on the boulevard whose lowest branch was perfect for supporting their tiny bodies and dangling legs. I had given them an assist up onto it before mowing the lawn. They watched me like two birds unruffled by the motion of man or machine. They were seated there still when I walked over to Ari.

"You know," he said, "all this manual labor is really cutting into your drinking time with me."

I took the beer from him, unscrewed the cap with my palm, and tipped the bottle toward him. "Cheers," I said.

Ari tapped my bottle with his, the *clink* reverberating between our houses.

I drank and thought of what to say next. Maybe ask about

his teaching, something we both had in common, but Ari also didn't strike me as one for small talk. If there was one thing I had picked up on in our few encounters, it was his aversion to any kind of unnecessary labor, forced conversation included. *Maybe we could talk about the kids*, I thought, as their giggles rained down like colorful leaves.

Ari took the lead in our awkward dance. "Simon likes Barbies," he said. I felt myself totter. A light wind in the day's decline stuck my sweat-stained shirt to my chest, and I forgot about the heat of the sun and the mower as autumn suddenly intruded on our moment.

"Is that a question?" I asked, my shoulders rising. "Or a statement?"

"Statement," he said. "That's the first thing I noticed about you two that day we met."

I wasn't sure how I felt about that. I tried to regain some balance by taking another swig of beer.

Ari, perhaps noticing a defensive shift in my body language, added, "It's cool, man. Said a lot about the two of you. A good first impression."

I relaxed a bit, my shoulders slackening, the beer again refreshing.

"Some parents aren't cool with that kind of shit, you know?" he said. *Shit*, for most people, but especially Ari, had multiple connotations, and I inferred its usage here as a positive. As he continued talking, his right hand made a chopping motion like he was some sensei about to split a board. "People have these rigid ideas about masculinity and femininity."

My mind returned to the graduate class on queer theory I'd taken at the university the semester before Simon was born. I'd been asked to serve as advisor to my school's Gender Sexuality Alliance (GSA) club, and I thought the course would help me understand the job. I was not prepared for the challenges to my thinking (in terms of upsetting a belief in binary systems like masculine/feminine) or how it would foreshadow my situation as a parent five years later. I most vividly recall reading Judith Butler's work, an American philosopher noted for her theories on gender and a theorist Ari also cited in his anthropology classes. In particular, her idea that gender is a performative act, and that performance is a fragile one, always in danger of being undone.

Back in high school, a friend of mine—the stereotypical jock, an athlete's body and ability to bed any girl he smiled at, or so he claimed—spent the night at my place. We pulled out the hide-a-bed within the couch and fell asleep watching "dirty" movies, ones starring Sylvia Kristel or Sybil Danning, on late-night cable television, the end tables a muddle of soda cans and rumpled potato chip bags. Sometime in the night I felt his body re-position itself as if to spoon with my own. He tossed his arm over me, found my nipple, and began fondling it. I pushed his arm off and scooted closer to the edge. He mumbled incoherently and turned on his other side. No mention was made of the incident in the morning. Maybe it was the memory of some long-forgotten high school conquest, or maybe it was any one of the "spicy" scenes upon which his eyes had gorged before falling asleep that led to such lucid dreaming. Or maybe there was something else going on inside him which, if we had spoken about it, would have undone the masculine persona he had spent an entire adolescence cultivating. Regardless, I was beginning to understand, from experience, how even the most hetero/gender normative people had within them the possibility of queerness, how gender and sexuality were never as fixed as I sometimes thought or wanted to believe. As difficult as it was to admit, there was some part of me that recognized my friend's touch as sexual and even found it momentarily pleasurable.

And it wasn't just him. I dated a girl in high school who had a twin sister. This sister soon started dating Matt, another friend of mine. Apparently, Matt and I had been spending so much time at their parents' place that we had become an annoyance. On one particular Sunday, we received word that no boys were allowed over. Thinking ourselves clever, I borrowed a skirt from my incredulous sister, and Matt borrowed a dress, and we drove to their home in drag. Their parents laughed, and we were allowed to stay provided we continued to play out the visit as our "feminine" selves.

"What does it mean to be a boy or a girl, anyway?" I asked.

"Or men?" Ari said, referencing the two of us drinking beer over a fence line, the smell of cut grass and gasoline heavy in the air, discussing Judith Butler and gender theory.

I looked at Simon and Gita sitting in their tree. *Theory is one thing*, I thought. *When it's your kid, it's another.*

WALKER BETWEEN WORLDS

Following my ordeal in the hospital, I felt I needed to learn more about my biological parents' medical history, so I wrote to Wisconsin's Adoption Records Search Program. I sat at my computer and scrolled through my inquiry. I hovered the cursor over the Send button. Did I really want to invite more turmoil into my life? Hadn't ignorance suited me for thirty-six years? I contemplated deleting my words and closing the page. Adrienne watched me from the couch across the room, a cup of coffee steaming in her hands. I sighed and clicked the mouse.

The manila envelope arrived much sooner than I expected on a January afternoon in 2012. Too large for the mail slot, I retrieved it from the frozen porch steps and brushed a few stray snowflakes from its surface. Adrienne and I waited until Simon was asleep that night and then sat on our bed flipping through pages of material. Everything from recent questionnaires filled out by both of my birth parents to correspondence with Catholic Social Services in the 1970s to court documents making my adoption official was included. The "Family History" questionnaires revealed various cancers, heart disease, and Alzheimer's in the bloodline, but this barely registered in light of other facts. For example, I was born in Wilton, Wisconsin, population 511, a mere ninety-six miles from Eau Claire. I was originally named Kevin before my adoptive parents, Rick and Judy Patrie, rechristened me Andrew. And my birth parents, Lisa and Bill, reconciled a few years after I was born, got married, and had five more children. Five. An entire brood out there, and I didn't know them at all. Had we driven by each other on the interstate? Said "excuse me" as we passed each other in a convenience store? Experienced momentary déjà-vu in the mirror of the other's face?

"It says here your parents want to meet you," Adrienne said, handing me the page she was reading.

I took the page from her and shuffled it among the others. It had been months since I felt anemic following my blood loss, but I was suddenly a bit dazed, light-headed.

"How're you doing?" Adrienne asked.

"Overwhelmed." I slowly stood up to place the paperwork on the nightstand.

"Crazy to think you have brothers and sisters out in the world," she said.

I snapped off the light and slid in next to her.

"I wonder if you look more like bio mom or bio dad," she said, using her feet to push my cold feet away from her warm body.

I lay on my back. "The black sheep has no resemblance," I said.

I imagined her eyes rolling at that comment.

"Say I meet them," I said, my head beginning to clear. "Is that some kind of slight against my mom and dad?" I asked.

Adrienne flipped her body toward me. "It's just a visit," she said. "You're not moving in with them."

"What if I'm a huge disappointment?"

"Impossible," Adrienne kissed my cheek. "On second thought," she paused. I sensed her lips forming a mischievous smile.

"Maybe you should send me instead."

Before today, my birth parents had been an abstraction, a figment of the imagination, incapable of being seen, touched, or spoken to. Now, in the pages of these documents, Lisa and Bill began to assume flesh and blood. In truth, I was curious. I had known I was adopted for as far back as I could remember. This sometimes made for awkward conversations with kids on the playground who, upon learning of my situation, could think of nothing to say to me other than, "Sorry," as if adoption was a condition akin to leprosy. I did feel like an outcast at times, though, and this was hard to admit to Adrienne. I was still seeking to answer who I was and where I fit in. *Not so unlike Simon*, I thought. Maybe meeting my birth parents could help with these questions.

The next morning, I arrived early to work. I filled my translucent water cup to the brim—a parting gift from the hospital—and began composing an email: "I suppose there is no easy segue," I wrote. "I'll just come out and say it: my name is Andrew Patrie, and I was born to you 36 years ago …" It took almost all fifty minutes of my classroom prep time to finish two paragraphs and send them off.

A few days later, I was supervising a study hall. Most students had their heads down, earbuds in, their cell phones singing an electronic lullaby. My inbox dinged. I saw the subject line: "Adoption," my birth mother's name, Lisa, and for a moment I wondered what the hell I had gotten myself into. I clicked on the notification and opened her message. It began: "We hoped we'd hear from you. I cannot imagine how overwhelming getting all that information was for you …" Whatever misgivings remained were quickly melting in the warmth of her words. She suggested we meet at their home in Wilton. Home. I looked up at my students, who hadn't moved; meanwhile, something seismic shifted within me. I made plans to visit at the end of March, over spring break, shortly after my birthday.

The evening of my birthday we drove to my parents' place, my childhood home, the Patrie home, for dinner. They lived a couple miles from us in a neighborhood similar to ours: tree-lined streets and houses in a row. The overcast sky yielded only a dusting of snow, but my father had shoveled the driveway anyway, and the bare asphalt was a dull dark strip inside a frosted field of white. Our visit also had an ulterior motive: letting my parents know about the Wilton trip. While I had kept them in the loop regarding my search for information about my birth parents, they didn't yet know we were going to meet them. I had avoided the topic thus far because I felt weird telling my parents, these people who had loved and cared for and raised me as their only son, about it. Irrational as it was, I didn't want them to feel like I was selling off my family home and moving on to another.

My mother, the only person who could claim this title, even if she didn't give birth to me, had on a white sweater and jeans, an apron sashed to her waist, and she was bending to take the baked chicken from the oven when we arrived. She winced a bit with the action. She'd been complaining about her back recently, so I went to her side to help. She shooed me away.

Adrienne and Simon were still on the landing when my dad came up from the basement. He doffed his red ball cap and placed it on Simon's head, which disappeared down to his nose. "Well, he'll grow into it," my dad said, beaming at his grandson. He then took the hat off Simon, turned it upside down, sprinkled a few dollar bills in it like it was a collection basket, and extended the cap toward Simon. "College fund," he said, and Simon scooped up the money.

"What do you say, Simon?" Adrienne asked.

"Thank you," he said.

"He's too young to be worrying about college," my mother said, using tongs to transfer the meat to a serving tray.

"Never too early to start saving," my dad said and looked at me. I felt as if I'd suddenly morphed before him into a pile of money bags representing the tens of thousands of dollars I'd accrued in college debt by the time I graduated with only a teaching license to show for it.

"Dinner's ready," my mom said.

After my mom served a birthday cheesecake and Simon had wandered to the basement to draw and color, I brought up visiting my birth parents. "I was hoping for your support in this," I said. My dad got fidgety as if he could hear sirens signaling "emotional talk" incoming. He started to clear the dishes from the table—the first time I could ever remember him doing so. My mother was sitting across from me, sipping coffee with Adrienne. "I'd like to know how you feel about this," I said.

My dad had moved on to rinsing the plates in the sink. Another first. My mom smiled at me. "It's sweet of you to ask us," she said, "but what's important is how *you* feel about it." She set her cup down. I saw her wince again, her hand moving to massage her lower back.

"You okay, Mom?" I asked.

"Just getting old, kiddo," she said.

I felt a little lurch in my gut.

"If it's our blessing you're looking for," she continued, "you know you have it." She looked at my dad. "Right, Rick?" He turned and nodded, though I wasn't sure how much of the conversation he'd actually heard.

Adrienne wrapped her arms around my mother and squeezed. "You're the best, Judy."

"Just make sure we still get to see you on your birthday, okay?" my mother said. "And Christmas, too."

The weather was overcast and brisk the morning of our trip to Wilton. Branches rattled in the wind. The gale tugged at our pant legs. Adrienne kept pulling her hair from her mouth. We all threw sweatshirts on before embarking. I was nervous. Adrienne and I had told Simon we were seeing friends we hadn't seen for a long time. He was only five-and-a-half years old. He also had a close relationship with my parents who took care of him every Wednesday. We didn't want to confuse him.

Wilton is located in Monroe County, part of what is referred to as the Coulee Region of the state, a ninety-minute drive south of us and marked by narrow ridges and steep valleys. That morning, mist clung to the hillsides, so we traveled in a kind of gossamer light when the sun finally broke through the cloud cover. As we got closer to town, we passed threadbare family farms, cars abandoned in yards, billboards in Spanish. Slushy roads wound, rose, and fell with little warning in the March thaw. This was where my birth parents grew up, caroused, fell in and out of and back in love with each other. I tried but could not conjure myself as a child here: biking these roads, exploring these hills so different from the topography of Eau Claire.

I turned onto Lithium Road and approached the house as guinea fowl scattered over the gravel drive. It was massive: two stories of walnut yellow timber bisected by a large stone fireplace and chimney. A deck encircled the house from the second story, allowing a bucolic view of the property's grassy flatland and distant ridges beyond the tree line. I spied an ATV roaming one of the trails. Lisa and Bill emerged from the homestead to greet us.

"You ready?" Adrienne asked.

I looked back at Simon. "Sure," I said.

We stepped out of the car, and Simon hid behind my leg. I resisted the urge to scoop him up in my arms and use him as a distraction if things turned awkward. I held his hand instead.

Lisa moved toward us, her red windbreaker rippling. She was just over five feet tall, small build, honey blonde hair, and tungsten blue eyes behind her glasses. "It's so good to see you," she said, embracing me. "I've thought of you often. Especially in March." She stepped aside to welcome Adrienne and Simon. Bill came forward.

"Welcome to our home," he said, hugging me as well. He was a few inches taller than she, small boned but muscular beneath his plaid flannel jacket, brown eyes, a noticeable space between his two front teeth, and a dark herringbone cap atop his head.

Looking at them both, I strained for some resemblance to myself. Maybe Bill's eyes? In my head, I stretched their bodies to approximate my height. I composited their faces, one over the other. Nothing took.

"It's chilly. Come on inside," Lisa said.

Adrienne and Simon followed Lisa while I hung back with Bill. He pointed to a large outbuilding as we walked. There were two green garage doors behind which he worked on car and truck transmissions. He'd done well for himself, he said. Business was steady, but he could see the writing on the wall. "Everything's computers nowadays," he clarified. "Automakers expect you to pay to download their diagnostics. It's gonna put me out of business." I didn't know what to say other than I was sorry to hear that. Apart from a chest-beating moment I had after changing a flat tire on the interstate the summer Adrienne was pregnant with Simon, my relationship with cars was purely utilitarian. They got me from point A to point B. When the vehicle went haywire, I deferred to my dad or someone like Bill. *Funny, I thought. Both nature and nurture failed me in the automotive department.*

The house was spacious and bright. Immaculate. A configuration of wooden frames and tiled floors. The kitchen, dining, and living rooms were open and blended one into the other. There were many windows overlooking the yard. A couple glass doors allowed entry out to the deck. "How 'bout a tour?" Bill asked me. Adrienne followed Lisa into the kitchen. Simon found a granddaughter's dollhouse on the living room floor and crouched down to play. No one but me seemed to notice.

"Sure," I said, and we descended to the basement.

"Man cave," he said as the full room came into view. There was a pool table in the corner, a big screen TV, the walls a race to see which could multiply faster: taxidermied deer heads or Wisconsin Badgers football tchotchkes. "Ever been to Camp Randall?" he asked. I shook my head. "We're season ticketholders. If you're ever interested …"

"Thanks. That's very kind."

"You want something to drink?" he asked. "Beer?"

I tried to remember the last time I drank before noon. Today seemed as good an occasion as any. "Please," I said.

Bill grabbed two beers from a nearby mini-fridge, and we continued the tour.

He led me to another room, flipping a switch in what I assumed was an office. The fluorescent lights ticked on and hummed. Row upon black metallic row of guns. "You hunt?"

I took a hunter safety course in seventh grade to fill an elective slot but also to try and fit in. Many of the boys in my grade hunted with their fathers. I remembered shooting a .22 long rifle at targets in a range off one of the shop classrooms. Hard to imagine that today, with active shooter drills happening every month in the school where I teach. It was the first and last time I fired a gun. "My dad didn't hunt, which means I didn't hunt."

Bill looked at me and shrugged and then switched off the lights.

Strike three, I thought. I didn't fault him. He was nervous and simply reaching out, trying to connect, not unlike my dad did with me through his passion for sports or the way I tried to get Simon to sit through some black-and-white horror movie. We are who we are. For better or worse. I was struck by the lack of questions about me, about my interests. I never much cared for the spotlight anyway, but it did lend a bizarre rhythm to the morning: the two of us standing together, him *not* asking about me. But I'd come to Wilton to learn about him and Lisa, and in learning about them, maybe I'd learn a little about myself, too.

We came back upstairs, and I could hear Adrienne laughing with Lisa in the kitchen. I caught her eye and she mouthed, *Everything okay?* I nodded and then followed Bill through the living room and out one of the glass doors to the deck. He pointed to a pond within yelling distance of the house, said there were fish in it, poles in the garage if I was interested. "Me and my brother," he said, "used to fish all the time when we were younger. Some of my best memories." He then recounted a story intended to be funny but whose punchline hit too close to home. How he and his brother came running with cane poles from their grandfather's farmhouse to the creek along the property line, flush with fish, or so they hoped. He caught a turtle, instead, and yanked the line so fast he found himself face to snapping face with it. The fear of ending up like some character in a two-reeler comedy, flailing and flopping with a reptile hanging off the tip of his nose, sent him careening. He fell backward into a pile of cow dung. His clothes were filthy. Once he was inside, clean and toweled dry, he realized he hadn't remembered to bring an extra pair of shorts or a shirt. His grandfather insisted they couldn't take him home covered in manure, and the only thing around to change into was an oversized women's dress. "I was like a brook trout hiding amidst the reeds," he laughed, "and no amount of bait was gonna get me out looking like that." Bill was red-faced, his eyes watering. I glanced through the glass at Simon, still playing with the dollhouse, swapping one dress on a figurine for another. "Can you imagine?" Bill asked. I turned back to face him. "A boy in a dress?"

I looked again at Simon. *Yes*, I thought. *I can.*

Lisa interrupted the moment with a call to lunch.

We gathered around the kitchen table helping ourselves to brats, burgers, and ears of sweet corn. Simon had a hot dog drowned in ketchup. Adrienne prompted Lisa and Bill between bites to fill in the backstory of how they met. Both of them recalled a fortuitous first encounter in a high school study hall. Lisa confided her attraction to Bill had much to do with his "bad boy" persona, and he asserted she was "the prettiest girl in the county." They addressed the relationship going on hiatus between 1975 and 1978, within which time I was born and my birth father joined the military. Listening to them talk, I realized the earlier exclusion of me from the conversation wasn't intentional, wasn't some kind of affront. It was two parental figures trying to make up for lost time. I did manage to break in occasionally and share about how Adrienne and I met, my teaching, my love of scary movies. After mentioning the latter, Lisa said, "You need to meet our oldest. She loves all things horror. She takes a week off work for Halloween."

Simon looked up from his hot dog and said, "There you go, Dad. Someone to watch those movies with."

After lunch, Lisa said she had some photos she wanted me to look at. I followed her to a bedroom. She removed a photo album from a shelf in the closet and laid it on the floral print bedspread. The pages bulged within. She flipped through them, and I stared at photographs from a life that could have been mine but was not. I tried to imagine myself on the back of an ATV or kneeling behind a deceased buck and lifting its lethargic neck by the antlers. She flipped further back in time to pictures of her parents. I pointed to her father. He was my height, my build: long and thin as a candlestick. No one in my family—not my parents, not my birth parents, not my siblings—looked anything like me. Here, at last, was a physical resemblance. "That's your grandfather," she said. "He lived to be eighty-one. Died of Alzheimer's and prostate cancer." She closed the album and returned it to the closet shelf. "They were decent people," she said, "but they were also God-fearing and rigid."

She told me about her pregnancy at fifteen years old, the ensuing scandal, which grew along with her belly, getting kicked out of her house, being ostracized from her family, and carrying me to term in a home for unwed mothers. Accommodations were spartan: a bed, desk, and chair. She remembered a cat that often wandered in, that would perch upon that desk and watch me move within her belly. "He was very interested in my little Kevin," she said. At the mention of my former name, a blush of embarrassment lit her cheeks. She looked at me as if seeking absolution. "It all comes back as if it was yesterday."

"I can't imagine what that was like for you."

She hesitated a moment before turning back to the closet and pulling out a large yellow envelope from within. "Now you can," she said. She read my face. "When you agreed to meet us,

I wrote some thoughts down, things I'd always wanted to say to you about that time." She handed the envelope to me. "Just don't read it in front of me, okay?"

I thought of her sacrifice thirty-seven years ago and thanked her for making the hard choice. The right choice. "I've had a good life," I said.

"That's more than I could've given you," she said, closing the closet door.

"But you did give it to me, in your way."

She looked at me, her eyes flickering a moment, and then she hugged me. "My heart is finally at peace," she whispered.

I could hear Simon giggling in the other room. "No," I heard him say to Adrienne, "this dolly goes here," and I wondered when I'd be able to feel a similar peace.

Lisa and Bill took us on a drive around Wilton, and we stopped for dinner at a German restaurant. It was nearly dusk when we returned to their home, and they walked us to our car. Adrienne and Simon said their goodbyes and then climbed in to give me a moment with my birth parents.

"Thank you both," I said. I was holding the envelope Lisa had given me. "For being so generous."

They both hugged me one last time. "Take care," they said.

I got behind the wheel and started the car. Adrienne brushed her fingers against my cheek. Lisa and Bill waved to us. I considered the dichotomy from which I sprang: I was Rick and Judy Patrie's son, but I was also an orphan from this Wilton clan. A walker between worlds. I wondered if this was how Simon felt, too. I knew I would've been even more of a pariah had I grown up in Wilton. It made me thankful that Eau Claire, with a population of 68,187, was large enough to increase the odds of running into more people like me or, at the very least, to allow for more anonymity. Perhaps there was hope here for

Simon, as well. As our car pulled away from my birth parents, I watched the evening draw down like a curtain over those hills, which were not a cradle, rolling like a lover's shoulders finally away from me.

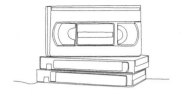

CHECKING IN, CHECKING OUT

The week following my visit to Wilton, I went out with a friend to a favorite bar from our youth. Thirty minutes into my story of meeting my birth parents, maybe half a drink, I received a text from Adrienne: "Andy, it's your mom." I apologized to my friend, threw enough money on the counter to cover the round, and said I'd call to reschedule with him. I shouldered open the door to the street and phoned Adrienne back. "Hey," I said.

"Hey. They're taking your mom to Rochester."

On some level I knew this call was coming. My mother's back had been bothering her for weeks. She finally got an appointment here in town, and Adrienne explained that someone didn't like the look of a scan from the lab. My mother was immediately taken by ambulance to the Mayo Clinic in Rochester, Minnesota. My father followed in his vehicle. I had a vision of my mother alone in the back of that ambulance, her body jolting with every pothole, every sudden turn. I would eventually hear that a former student, just coming off a twelve-hour shift, volunteered to sit with my mother as they transported her because he recognized her last name. Turns out he was in my study hall years ago. He remembered how I used to play heavy metal music on the boom box as he filed into my room. "He was a cool guy," he told her. "Least I can do is keep his mom company." These are life's strange, benevolent ripples.

My mother spent half her life wondering about me, worrying about me and how I'd turn out. Growing up, I was a peculiar kid, and not just because I was adopted. I was attracted to such alien art forms as heavy metal music and horror films. Among my peers in Eau Claire, there was scant interest in these things and zero understanding from the adults in my life, especially my mother.

In the summer of 1989, I was fourteen years old. The phone was ringing. I glanced at the digital clock in my bedroom: 11:00 a.m. My mom periodically called to check in on me whenever she was at work, and I was at home alone. I got out of bed, ran upstairs to the kitchen, and picked up the cordless phone. It wasn't my mother.

"You got the movie?" my friend, Pete, asked.

I could see him, his red hair and denim jacket, up hours before me, pacing the floor of his home, respecting my "summer hours" policy and letting me sleep in a bit longer. I walked back down to my room and plopped onto my bed.

"Yeah, I got it."

"You had no problem renting it?" he asked.

"No problem."

"Woo!" he rejoiced. "This is gonna be awesome!"

"Yeah," I yawned, shaking my head to wake up.

"We're finally gonna see it."

"Yeah." I rubbed my eyes.

"And no one's home at your house?" he asked.

"Not a soul until after four."

"Cool, dude. I'm on my way." He hung up.

I lowered my hand to the side of my bed and reached between the mattress and box spring. It wasn't porn. It was a battered VHS rental copy of *The Texas Chain Saw Massacre*. To my mother, though, there was no difference.

Films of this ilk had a fearsome reputation, a cancer-like quality my mother feared might take hold and rot my moral center (it was the same concern she had regarding my burgeoning interest in heavy metal music in the wake of Tipper Gore and the Parents Music Resource Center's "satanic panic" a few years earlier), which made seeing this movie an irresistible challenge. And so, the day before, I hoofed it the hilly quarter mile from our neighborhood to the Pick 'n Save to rent the tape while my parents were at work and my sister was away at camp. The blue of the sky seemed to fall in all around me, the asphalt became a shimmering lake that receded with every footfall, and the older clerk, who, in sharp contrast to my mother's prohibitions, perfunctorily checked me out and waved me on as long as I remembered to "Be kind. Always rewind."

Before chains like Blockbuster and Family Video dominated the market, we could rent videos at grocery stores and bait and tackle shops. Even U-Haul had a wall of tapes. No one cared about age restrictions. But that didn't make me feel any less guilty about going behind my mother's back. We were, after all, a good Catholic family. And my mother might've been right about the porn comparison. They weren't sex films but rather gory slasher films where the money shot was some hapless victim's cut throat and subsequent arterial spray. However, as if to counter any misgiving, *poof*, Pete's face appeared in my head, like the proverbial devil on the shoulder, saying, "Dude, part of being a good Catholic *is* sinning."

It was also a gorgeous, late summer day in Wisconsin, a place Shakespeare could have been talking about when he penned the line: "And summer's lease hath all too short a date." Other friends were out riding their bikes to the river downtown two miles away. But this was an activity meant for the dark. And Pete and I only had the day, so we'd do our best to seal ourselves in the artificial night a basement bedroom provides, especially since my only window looked out underneath our deck.

I heard the side door bang open, and Pete was down the steps and into my room in a seemingly single bound. He dumped a bag of Cool Ranch Doritos in my lap and cracked a condensing can of Mello Yello.

I held the tape aloft like some rare jewel prized from a mine.

"Commence with the massacring," he said, settling into the chair next to my bed.

I slid the tape in and pressed PLAY. The tracking adjusted, and the FBI warning flickered past. I snapped off the lights and closed the blinds. There was no turning back from this thing.

"Aw yeah," Pete said. "Here we go."

It took thirty minutes to get to the first kill. Some guy in jeans and a T-shirt opened to expose his hairy chest got hit with a hammer to the head, the blow delivered by a hulking figure wearing a mask of dried human skin. "Whoa!" we said and exchanged grins over the television light.

The scene shifted outside to the guy's girlfriend rocking on a swing. She stood up, and the camera moved with her, tracking beneath the swing, following her progression toward the idyllic white farmhouse where she would die.

The phone rang.

I paused the tape.

"Aw, man," Pete moaned.

I knew it was my mom, as if she'd held off on calling until she knew I was up to no good. I grabbed the cordless and left the room.

"Everything okay?" she asked.

I swore she could see through that receiver.

"Just fine," I said. "Pete stopped over. We might play some *Zelda*."

"Pete's over?" There was a flutter in her pitch, momentarily revealing her disdain, followed by an attempt to sound neutral again.

She and Pete had history. I still had the contraband Metallica tape he made for me earlier that summer. A cassette-to-cassette dub of their recently released fourth album, *...And Justice for All*. I remember cranking that tape in my bedroom while my parents were outside doing yard work. I was no more than a couple minutes into album opener "Blackened" when I looked up to find my mother, an imposing former farm girl, filling the doorway as vocalist James Hetfield barked: "See our mother put to death, see our mother die." I clumsily searched for the STOP button on my boom box. "Mom," I said, a pubescent squeak present in my voice, "it's about the environment. You know, Mother Nature?" I pointed at her gloved hands, earth-caked from pulling weeds. "How we should treat her better." She demanded to know where I'd gotten the tape, and I had to give up Pete's name. She called his father later that night.

"Yep," I said, shaking loose from the memory. "Pete's here, and ..."

I could see Pete now pacing in my room.

"Well, don't stay inside all day. It's lovely out," she said. "I don't think you appreciate what a gift summer is. Oh, if our roles were reversed ..."

I saw Pete walking toward me. "Dude," he said, loud enough for my mom to hear on the other end, "pausing it this long is bad for the tape."

My eyes bulged.

"Tape?" my mother asked. "What tape?"

"Yeah, uh, gotta go, Mom. Love you," I said.

"Are you watching that chainsaw movie?" she asked. "The one I forbid you to see?"

I had been pestering her for weeks to let me see it before Pete finally talked me into renting it without her consent. Then, not a peep out of me about the movie, just radio silence on my end, which only kindled her suspicions.

"I'll be taking my lunch soon, and I'll be eating at home today," she said. My mother did secretarial work at the time for Johnson Litho Graphics, literally down the hill from our home. "There better be no evidence of that tape in my house when I get there. Understand?"

I wanted to say yeah, I understand. I understand you make it tough to be a rebel. Instead, I said, "Yes, Mom."

"And no Pete, either."

"Yes, Mom."

I hung up the phone.

"Nice one," I said to Pete.

"Sorry, dude."

"Whatever," I said. "You gotta go. And I gotta get the movie back to Pick 'n Save before she gets home for lunch."

On his way out the door, Pete said, "There's always next summer."

I thought of saying, "Maybe we could do it at your house next summer," but he was already gone.

I returned to my bedroom and stared at the TV a moment before ejecting the tape. The image still paused on the girl about to enter that idyllic white farmhouse where she would die. For the moment, though, she was oblivious and beautiful amidst the deep green foliage and soft clouds sweeping the sky.

Adrienne and I arrived in Rochester the following morning after leaving Simon with our friends. My sister, Nikki, and her husband, Jim, had already joined my father in the waiting room. The doctor held up an MRI image to us. He pointed out the tumor, which looked like a naked snail now using my mother's spine as a new shell. I thought of how pale her bones were in that photo, like the moon, though not as remote, and soon we were tethered in a kind of orbit around her bedside. However, this time it was my turn to wonder and worry about her and the slasher film playing out inside her at the cellular level. "It's going to be okay," she told all of us.

Surgeons removed the tumor on her spine and treated the area with radiation. This greatly relieved the strain on her back. However, the cancer's point of origin was her pancreas. Doctors discovered two inoperable tumors there, slowly growing, and we were informed they could be kept in check with a monthly shot, affording my mother precious years instead of weeks. "No need to plan the funeral just yet," the nurse said.

And so we didn't. We knew my mother would keep up with her treatments, and life would resume as it had before we came to that awful, beautiful clinic. She would continue to host every family gathering, plant her garden every summer, and decorate the house every holiday. If only looking at the surface, one could forget there was any cancer present at all. But we knew it was there, waiting, lurking like that hulking maniac inside the farmhouse.

WHAT WOULD YOU DO?

Three years later, and Simon was eight. I was carrying a plate of sandwiches from the kitchen to the living room when I heard him. "That's me," he said. "I'm transgender." I stopped mid-stride. Outside, two neighbor boys tossed a football back and forth in the street. One boy overshot the other, and the ball spiraled out of his reach. It hit the pavement and wobbled like my legs at that moment.

I sat down next to Simon on the couch—he was outfitted in his favorite blue dress—set the sandwich plate on the coffee table next to us, and watched him watch an ABC News program titled *What Would You Do?* I don't know how he found the show, but there it was. The hidden camera show conducted social experiments to see how bystanders would react to dramatic interactions in the most innocuous places: restaurants, retail stores, hair salons. The scenario prompting Simon's response involved the latter location. A young girl wanted to cut her hair short, like a boy, while her mother resisted. "Girls have long hair," her mother said. Hidden cameras caught the reactions of the surrounding patrons in the salon. There was a woman beneath a hair dryer and a man seated to the girl's right getting a haircut, both stealing glances at the mother and child.

The program had Simon rapt, so I stared at his hair, its "just got out of bed" fuzziness, and imagined it growing beyond his shoulders, reaching to the middle of his back. He said, "Dad, they said a word. 'Transgender.' I think they're talking about me."

"Why do you think that, buddy?" I asked. I tried to play it cool. Deep inside, though, I could feel the bottom starting to drop from under me.

"This girl," he said, pointing at the screen, "believes she's really a boy."

"What does that mean to you?"

The couch cushions shook in his urgency to tell me.

"It means I'm a boy who's really a girl," he said. "Transgender."

Things that happen out of nowhere really don't. There is always an antecedent, some precipitating event. Yet we are still stunned senseless by cancer diagnoses, automobile collisions, our own frangible hearts. The dress from his playroom, the Barbies on the shelf, his fairy wings at the lake those years ago weren't some phase. All the dots were connecting in a way I could no longer deny.

In the last few years, there had been other changes, too. Gone was his fleeting interest in the kind of rough-and-tumble play that had been impressed upon me by my father. When I was little, my dad would get down on all fours at one end of the hallway, in front of the door to my bedroom, while my sister, Nikki, and I would get on our haunches at the other end, near the kitchen, and then we'd sprint at him, attempting to get by and into the "end zone" of my darkened room. I didn't care about the game as much as I did the physical affection of my father's arms. I tried to recreate a version of this play in our basement. Adrienne would sit on the couch and act as cheerleader while I positioned myself at the farthest wall from the staircase. Simon would start at the stairs and come bolting at me, and I would collapse on top of him until we were a tangle of limbs and laughter. Now, he would rather play at being a mermaid, and the couch was shore, and if Adrienne or I fell to the ocean floor of our carpet, he would swim down to rescue us.

Year by year, there were words we'd dare not speak for fear speaking them would make them real. We'd never used the word "transgender" around him, never acknowledged it when it tried nudging its way into our conversations. "Maybe he's just gay," we'd say. I'd seen same-sex couples openly holding hands in the hallways of the high school where I taught, and earlier that summer the Supreme Court had affirmed the right of same-sex couples to marry in all fifty states.

I told myself it wasn't an issue of gender but rather a concern for his safety, a desire for his acceptance. Going forward, this declaration of transgender would impact friendships, relationships—everything. In Andrew Solomon's book *Far from the Tree*, published in 2012, there is a chapter called "Transgender." One of the many things he discusses is the violence and the exile these kids face. In citing "a large survey" conducted in 2009 by the National Center for Transgender Equality and the National Gay and Lesbian Task Force, Solomon writes, "Four out of five people surveyed had been harassed or physically or sexually attacked in school, almost half by teachers … More than half of trans youth have made a suicide attempt, as opposed to 2 percent of the general population. The rates of substance abuse and depression are staggering. Some 20 to 40 percent of homeless youth are gay or trans."[1] Simon's gender identity could lead to his suffering. And that, more than anything, was what we felt we must protect him from.

"Dad?" Simon said, tugging me from my thoughts.

---

1 Andrew Solomon, *Far from the Tree: Parents, Children and the Search for Identity* (Scribner, reprint 2013).

"Huh?"

"Can I have some chips?" he asked, halfway through his sandwich.

"Sure," I said and stood up.

"Dad?"

"Yes?"

"Are you going to tell Mom? About me being a transgender?"

I imagined Adrienne out running her errands, taking some time for herself. I said, "We'll talk more about this when she gets home, Simon." Saying his name felt suddenly important: it was a word we could not stop saying for fear it would otherwise disappear, fragile as the very breath with which we uttered it.

"Good," he said and returned to his sandwich.

By the time Adrienne got home, he'd grown bored with the TV and gone up to his room. I mentioned the *What Would You Do?* program to her and Simon's declaration of transgender. She was ready to charge upstairs to speak with him about this, but I convinced her to wait, to table the conversation, to see if he'd bring it up again. Against her better judgment, Adrienne relented, and things were quiet for two months—right up until Simon's ninth birthday when I found myself, again, caught in a rerun.

As a transgender kid, he demanded he should be able to wear his dress.

But I told him he couldn't wear the dress that day.

"It's my birthday," he protested. "I should get to do what I want. I'm nine now."

It was a Saturday afternoon, and Simon was sunken before us on our living room couch, sulking in his swim trunks. Rachel and Gita were waiting in the kitchen. He'd insisted Gita ride with us to the party. By this time our families were comfortable enough to allow our dramas to play out in front of each other.

"I know," I said, "but—"

"But you said, 'We'll see.' Remember?"

I honestly did not remember and turned to Adrienne, who threw up her arms as if to say, "Don't look at me."

"That was before you decided on a waterpark for your birthday," I said. "Besides, you'll just get it wet. Some other time, okay?"

Simon began picking at random fuzz balls along the upholstery.

"Look," I said, "Gita's waiting. Your friends will be arriving at the waterpark soon. You don't want to be late to your own party, do you?"

He shook his head, avoiding eye contact.

"Good," I said, spared for the moment. "Let's get going."

I scooped up the car keys from the dining room table and followed Adrienne to the kitchen. Gita was by the sink in her one-piece bathing suit and sandals. She carried a tote bag stuffed with a towel, a change of clothes, and a gift for Simon. "Ready?" Adrienne asked her, and Gita shot her a thumbs up.

"Everything *pool?*" Rachel asked Adrienne, trying to lighten the mood. A lawyer by trade, she was pragmatic yet kind and also something of a pun aficionado.

Simon trailed behind us toward the side door.

"We'll see," Adrienne said.

I waited for him to pass. He was muttering to himself. I only caught a fragment. "Some birthday," he said. I locked the door behind us.

Ten minutes later, we arrived at Chaos Indoor Waterpark: tropical humidity, serpentine slides, and a tumult of voices in surround sound. The other parents greeted us, gave us sympathetic smiles, and then took off for a few hours of respite. Eight kids were now tailing Simon, their little heads soon popping between the holes of the inner tubes in the lazy river.

"Like whack-a-mole," I said. Adrienne nudged me in the side.

My wife and I entered the party tent set up by the waterpark attendants along an edge of the lazy river and uncovered seats beneath towels, gift bags, and flip-flops. We sat and watched the people float by.

"So ..." Adrienne said.

"So ..." I said.

"You want to talk about the dress?"

I didn't.

I watched an unmanned tube float by in the current of the lazy river. It felt like a symbol for our life: uncoupled from its mooring and starting to drift. Two months ago our son had identified himself as transgender. He now wanted to wear a dress in public. I admit I was insecure over what Simon's dress-wearing said about our parenting. Would a passerby simply smile and offer a kind, "Good for you"? Or would I end up chest to chest with some red-faced guy shouting vulgar epithets at our son?

Adrienne re-phrased her question, "Any guess as to how this day is going to go?"

Simon and a couple friends drifted by. I had just enough time to ask how they were doing.

The friends presented two glistening thumbs up while Simon floated on.

"It's a birthday party," I said to Adrienne. "What kid doesn't have fun at a birthday party?"

It wasn't long before the birthday tent was littered with signs of the famished: abandoned pizza crusts, emptied solo cups, frosting-smeared plates, gift bags with their decorative insides pulled out. "So far, so good," I said to Adrienne as I attempted to herd Simon's gifts into a corner of the table. The kids had gone back to the water.

Another couple and their two children, a boy and a girl, sat down at a table next to our tent, the mother's blonde hair up in a bun and the father's muscled chest barely contained beneath his T-shirt, a quintessential nuclear family. He and I made eye contact. It felt like a hard, high school locker room stare, and I thought I knew about him, the dozens like him, jocks and bullies from my youth, and then Gita approached us.

"Um ... Simon's upset," she said.

"What about?" Adrienne asked.

"Dunno, but he's in the lazy river. Crying."

Adrienne and I moved to the landing and waited for the current to bring him around again.

"How are you, sweetheart?" Adrienne asked.

"Terrible," he replied.

"Let's get you out of there, okay?" she said.

"NO!" he shouted and sailed on.

We helped file the other kids out to their towels.

I checked my phone. Fifteen minutes to go until parent pickup.

Adrienne said, "He won't get out."

"It's a birthday party," I repeated, this time so Simon would hear. "What kid doesn't have fun at a birthday party?"

I was at a loss as to how to get him out of the water without creating a bigger scene when I saw Rachel. She had a large green pool bag slung over her left shoulder. She'd come for Gita and to see if we needed help with anything.

"Simon's having a meltdown. I thought things were cool, but ..." I stopped.

Rachel went to speak with Adrienne while I tended to the other children. Together they coaxed Simon from the water. Adrienne wrapped him in a towel, and he headed off to a corner of the tent.

"What did you say to get him out?" I asked.

"It was all Rachel," Adrienne said. "She brought a dress he can wear. He's okay now."

I thought back to our house earlier that afternoon, Rachel's hesitancy to leave, her concern.

"I hope I didn't overstep," she said, tucking the empty pool bag under her arm.

"God, no," Adrienne said. "You're a lifesaver."

Simon emerged from the tent, smiling, billowing in the dress's soft, thin fabric.

However, as we passed in front of that nuclear family next to us, I was afraid of what they might say. And of what I might do in response. Their eyes were on Simon, and I felt my whole body going morgue-stiff. I inched in front of Simon, shielding him from a world I knew but wouldn't admit he must inhabit.

They averted their eyes from our happy boy in his dress. I thought about how Simon being transgender would mean more moments like this one, how being in the "wrong" clothes, so to speak, would become part of our reality. Andrew Solomon writes, "Whenever I saw someone who looked like a middle-aged man in a dress, I felt an ache. In a child, the effect was curiously transfixing, as though he had just imagined himself into being." Yet Simon was not at all aware of the situation around him. He didn't care (or notice) who was judging him. Being a girl was more important to him.

As I walked by, the father stood up and, with exaggerated effort, slowly pulled off his shirt. His biceps flexed. One prominent vein snaked and pulsed. His chest was hairless, revealing amateur looking tattoos, a blue scrawl of children's names, Mia and Aaron, one for each pectoral. I halted and waited, almost daring him to say something, and then Adrienne called out that the other parents had arrived.

At the front entrance we matched the kids with their parents and said thank you and goodbye while Simon lingered in his dress next to Gita, who was now similarly apparelled. I kept looking back at the guy. Sensing the tension, Rachel offered to take Simon with her and Gita for a couple hours so Adrienne and I could talk. Our dear friend to the rescue, again. How incredibly lucky were we to live next to such an open-minded and supportive family?

"You be good, okay?" I said. "Listen to Rachel."

"Yes, Dad,"

I bent down and kissed him on top of his wet head and whispered, "Happy birthday, Simon."

"Thanks, Dad." The automatic door *whooshed* open then and swirled him and the dress away.

Adrienne and I decamped to a nearby bar in what was once Eau Claire's cannery district. The area was slated for redevelopment. The bar was the only building not abandoned or awaiting demolition. It was now fall and chilly at dusk, but we still sat opposite each other at one of the outdoor picnic tables. The sky was a pastel smear of pink and blue. Adrienne had paid for the beer, two generous pours that colored our glasses a rusty sunset and ran over each rim. I took a pull; it went down only slightly bitter.

"You're holding tight to something," she said, looking straight through me. "What's on your mind?"

I waited for a moment and then blurted out, "How do I know what was in his heart?"

Adrienne sipped at her beer, coughing a little. "Who are you talking about?"

"The dude," I stammered. "At the waterpark. The tattoos."

"I have no idea who you are talking about."

"You didn't see him? The family next to our tent as we were leaving? He kept staring at Simon."

"I was too busy with Simon to notice," she said.

I looked at what remained of the surrounding cannery district, ruinous in the failing light. "Seems like that's all I notice anymore."

Adrienne touched my arm. "We can't protect him from the world forever."

"But that dude took his shirt off right in front of me," I said. "Flashing the tattoos of his kids' names. Totally aggressive."

"Or," Adrienne countered, "he was letting you know he's a father, too. One who loves his children enough to ink their names into his chest."

"So?"

"So you're a father who loves his son enough to let him wear a dress."

The crickets were out, their song as sharp as the stars in the cold night.

"Not everybody in this world means to hurt our child," Adrienne said.

I thought of those men around their fire pit that fairy wing summer.

"There are also people like Rachel, Ari, and Gita in it," she continued. "We have to stop seeing the worst in people, or that's all Simon will see, too."

I returned my gaze to the darkness now gathered over her shoulder and strained my eyes beyond it.

STORM WARNING

A few days after Simon's ninth birthday party, Adrienne pulled me into his bedroom one afternoon and shut the door. He was downstairs watching the same episode of *What Would You Do?* She handed me a leopard print journal, "Love Never Fails" in calligraphy on the cover. We had picked it up for him at the Books-A-Million in town.

"Have you been going through his journal?" I asked.

"It was just lying open on his bed," she said, and then she added, "Like he wanted someone to see it."

I flipped through pages of third-grade ephemera: who's crushing on who, drama with a girl one year above. Adrienne stopped my hand on page 11. The passage read:

Now let me tell you a little about myself. Hi my name is Graceful Alexander Patrie. And before you ask my real name is Simon. I am transgender. Here is a drawing of me with long hair.

In the drawing beneath the words, his hair was dark, lush, down to his waist. His lips were full. Eyelashes long. Breasts pushed from underneath the dress he attired himself in.

"What do you think?" Adrienne asked.

I searched for a punchline to break the tension. I thought of an after-school evening playing a basketless game of "Horse" on the elementary school lot; Simon riding his bike down the sidewalk, training wheels clacking over the grooves in the concrete, and him still tipping over despite the support; a kickball soaring over his head while he tracked the progress of a butterfly in the outfield. I said, "I think Simon is anything but graceful." Adrienne cracked up, her head filling with her own memories, though it was a nervous laughter we shared, the kind where we could have just as easily wept.

"I think he's serious," she finally said.

"Me too."

"We need to talk to a professional," she said. "About how to navigate this."

"Agreed."

A couple of weeks later, we fretted in the waiting room of a therapist recommended to us by Simon's pediatrician. The room was warm. There were magazines on end tables and children's toys in a corner, but the brick building and cold autumn light seeping in from the high windows still felt institutional. I held Adrienne's hand while Simon scrolled through my phone apps. We told him, prior to our arrival, that in light of all the recent changes in our family, we felt it was healthy to talk to someone, a professional. Simon, for his part, just rolled with it, mostly ambivalent. When his name was called, we all stood to meet the therapist as she walked in. She was dressed in a sweater and slacks, fall colors. Frizzy brunette hair brushed her shoulders. Ann's smile was kind. "If you don't mind," she said, "I'm going to borrow Simon for a bit, and we're going to go play."

"Um, sure," I said.

Simon handed me my phone and slid off the chair. He looked back at us and then followed her down the hall to her office. I overheard the therapist compliment Simon on the dress he was wearing. Since the waterpark incident we had reached a family truce allowing him to wear a dress outside of home on certain occasions and at certain locations.

"I was expecting that to be way more awkward," Adrienne said.

Within thirty minutes we were ushered back to the therapist's office. She was seated near a desk cluttered with papers and books—the chaos of professional life. A window looked out on another oatmeal-stone building. Simon was seated at a small, round table, drawing a picture. We sat down on a couch opposite the therapist, and I resisted saying, *I thought you were supposed to lie down on one of these.* She jotted something on a legal pad.

"Honestly," she began, "when you made the appointment, I had no idea how to approach this."

Adrienne and I glanced at each other.

"But I did some research, and here's what I know." She leaned toward us. "There's nothing wrong with Simon."

We both exhaled heavily.

"I know you already know that," she said. "You're here to figure out how to move forward as a family."

Adrienne nodded.

"Tell me about Simon," she said.

We held nothing back. Ann listened and took notes. When we finished, she reclined in her chair and asked, "How is Simon socially?"

"Very social," Adrienne said. "He's never had a problem interacting with other kids."

"How is school going?"

"He's doing well academically. No concerns from any of his teachers."

"I'd say that's a credit to both of you," she said. "You've given him space, love, and support. You don't have a troubled kid, mentally or otherwise."

We all looked to Simon, content with his crayons.

"Lots of children exhibit gender nonconformity at some point," she continued. "It's only a small percentage of children who identify as transgender at Simon's age who actually pursue it into adolescence and then adulthood. Give him the space to pivot back if he changes his mind. The last thing you want to do is paint him into a corner."

She placed her notepad on her desk and scooted her chair closer to us.

"You're going to have some decisions to make in the next couple years as puberty approaches. For now, though, let him be who he is." She turned and shuffled some papers on her desk before adding, "I'd be wary of only celebrating this part of him. For example, I'd advise against presenting him to people as 'our transgender child.'"

"Oh, you don't have to worry about that," I said.

Adrienne shot me a look.

A half hour later, as I guided the car out of the parking garage, my head felt like a wheel, ever spinning. The ride was mostly silent save for the metronome of the turn signal. Simon was in the back, saying nothing, occupied with the houses we passed and the Halloween décor, lights shining from windows turning facades into giant jack-o'-lanterns. Adrienne asked him what he thought of the therapist. "She's really nice," he said. "I hope I can talk with her again."

"That's great to hear, honey," she said. "Your dad and I like her, too."

It was true; she was approachable, intuitive, and smart, but our conversation left me disquieted. After arriving home, I climbed upstairs to our bedroom while Adrienne heated up some noodles for Simon. She soon joined me.

"How are you?" she asked.

"More confused than I was."

She sat down on the bed beside me.

"So is this what we're going with from now on?" I asked. "Our son is transgender? Even though he could change his mind down the road?"

"We are letting him wear dresses out in public now, so ..."

"A dress is one thing," I said, "but this ..."

"I'm not so sure the two are mutually exclusive."

"What do you mean?" I asked.

"I mean, they both have to do with seeing yourself as something other than you are," she said. "Or maybe seeing yourself as you really are."

I thought about Simon when he was my little Lon Chaney, my kid with one thousand faces.

She continued, "Simon doesn't see himself as Simon."

"He's our boy. What do you think the world will do to him if we send him out into it like this?"

"Perhaps that's not our call to make," she said.

I thought, *What's not our call? That he's our boy?* But I said nothing, afraid of the answer I did not want to hear.

Adrienne took a breath. "You're not the only one to worry, Andy."

I could see the anxiety in her creased forehead and her slumped shoulders. She was the center of our family, our rock, but the night after "finding" Simon's journal she stopped sleeping. After a week of no sleep, I compelled her to call Urgent Care. They prescribed her some medication, which seemed to help, at least with the sleeping part.

"I feel like I change my mind every day," she continued, "about what we're doing, how we're doing it, if we're doing right by our child. Do we do this thing that could potentially fuck up our kid's life? Adolescence is already cruel enough."

"This just feels like a whole other level," I said. "I'm not ready for it."

Adrienne reached for my hand and said, "I think he's in that small percentage the therapist spoke about. I really do." She used her free hand to wipe her eyes. "Regardless," she continued, "this is uncharted territory, and I'm not ready for it, either." She paused. "But maybe Simon is."

There were storms in the forecast. Clouds were piling up inside our home as well: Simon's coming out to us as transgender, our visits with the therapist, our witching hour indecision over what we should do. And I just wanted to forget about it all. At least for a little while. *I deserve a night out*, I thought. As if Adrienne didn't. As if she couldn't feel the weight of the world centering on her shoulders. I grabbed my car keys from the kitchen counter and left in a huff. She called after me, "When will you be home?" I let the side door close on the question.

I hesitated beneath the white eaves of our home and thought, *I do not recognize myself at this moment. Then again there's so much about my life I don't recognize anymore.* I almost turned around and walked back in. An apology on my lips like a kiss. Instead, I swallowed all I was feeling, like a shot, got in the car, and drove to the nearest bar for the evening.

On my way downtown, the wind picked up. Gold leaves whirled and plastered against my windshield, looking like tiny hands. I thought of Simon and then turned on the wipers.

I parallel parked between a compact car and an SUV. When I stepped out, I was too far from the curb. I could almost see my father shaking his head and hear him saying, "What are you doing, son?" I ignored it and crossed the street.

The soft thunder of the jukebox was perceptible before I pushed open the bar's green door to reveal a shadow world in that dim light, the brightest of which advertised various beers, whiskey, rum. Pick your poison. The next brightest was the television on the wall tuned to local weather. The radar showed a line of storms moving up from the south. Billiard balls broke across a pool table to my left.

I took in the rest of the room. Two guys played pinball near the bathrooms. Three girls tucked into their laughter in a far corner. Regulars ringed around the bar. It was a place without memory, separated from reality. I moved a stool so I could lean against the counter and better see the rows of bottles behind the barman. He was the only one working, and he surveyed the room like a beleaguered apothecary as he mixed several different bottles into a mason jar for the man sitting two chairs down from me. The glass layered with colors reminded me of a poster I saw in a science classroom, which showed the earth segmented from crust to core. The patron left cash on the counter in exchange for the elixir.

"What do you need?" he asked me while chucking some empty Coors bottles into a recycling bin near his feet.

A reset, I thought.

"A whiskey and Diet Coke."

"You got it."

I took my drink to an unoccupied table and sipped it through a neon yellow stir straw. Strong medicine. I felt it on an empty stomach. I closed my eyes and allowed my mind to wander.

"Patrie!" a voice shouted.

I opened my eyes to see a woman standing next to my table. It took a moment, but I recognized her as a former student. The guy she was with said something in her ear and then moved to the bar.

"Hey," I said as she came in for a hug. Her hair tickled my nose, and her perfume remained after the embrace.

"How long has it been?" she asked, sitting down across from me.

"Your graduation."

"That was ten years ago. It can't be that long."

She set her purse on the table and took off her jacket. She wore a white shirt, blue jeans, and open-toe sandals despite being late fall. She reached her hands over to clasp my own. "So, how have you been?"

I wasn't sure what to say. I was not expecting such forwardness, such vivacity, such beauty in a place like this tonight. "Um, fine. And you?"

"I'm great," she said, releasing my hands. "I'll be starting grad school soon out west. Working for the university in the meantime." She threaded her fingers through her hair and wrapped a tie around it. Her neck palely shone in the gloom, a bright moon enclouded. "What are you doing out alone? In this place?"

"Isn't that supposed to be my line?" I said, and she smiled. "I haven't been out, on my own, for a very long time, and I—"

Her friend returned, and he spoke to her while looking at me. "I left my ID at home, and that fucker won't serve me. We have to go back and get it."

"You go. I'll wait for you here."

"Are you serious?" he asked, breaking eye contact with me to stare at her.

"I just got settled. Why should I have to go back to your apartment because you forgot your ID?" She fished in her purse and pulled something out. "See? I have my ID. Patrie, do you have your ID?" I looked at my feet.

He turned from her to me and said, "Whatever."

As he exited, she scrunched her face at me. "Sorry."

"I'm okay," I said. "I just feel bad for your boyfriend."

She snorted and covered her mouth in embarrassment.

"Husband?" I said.

She snorted even louder. "Neither. Just a ... friend."

I smiled. "Well, friend, may I buy you a drink?"

"Thought you'd never ask."

I got up, her storm-gray eyes following me, her slight figure somehow capable of canting the room toward her.

She asked about my teaching, and I asked about what she'd be studying in grad school. The whiskey settled in. We laughed and hardly noticed when the rain began slapping against the windows. It had been a welcome reprieve from home life. Still, more than once, I glanced at the wedding band on my left hand, wondering about what Simon was doing while somehow managing to avoid bringing up anything about my family. When she did finally ask, I took a quick sip of my drink, looked around, and deflected, "You know, it sure is taking your friend a while to find that ID."

She cocked her head a bit and said, "Yeah. I don't think he's coming back."

I felt the lightning flash of her leg rubbing against my own underneath the table. We made eye contact, yet I did nothing to stop it.

"Do you want to do a shot with me?" she asked.

"Sure."

"Come on, then."

I followed her to the bar, where she ordered and paid for two shots. The liquid was clear and smelled strongly of peppermint. She *clinked* her glass against mine, and we each drank our own in one swallow. It burned.

"What was that?" I asked.

"Rumple Minze."

"It tastes like a candy cane on fire."

She said, "They say you're supposed to kiss someone after you do a shot of Rumple Minze."

"Ah, yes. The infamous *they*."

"But you're married." She said these words and then smiled in such a way that I understood this fact did not disqualify me from the kiss. She relaxed her shoulders, easing her back against the bar.

"I am," I said, hoping it didn't sound like an apology.

"Too bad," she sighed.

She looked up at me, those storm-gray eyes. I found myself staring at the red line of her lips, all the imagined possibilities, all the devastating consequences that came with crossing it. Suddenly, whether it was the angle of the room or the dizzying effect of the alcohol, I sensed myself leaning in for that kiss. There was an unreality to the moment, like a car coming at you in your lane. I could smell the mint on her lips, almost brush them with mine. Above her head, on the television, a meteorologist interrupted. *Thunderstorm warning*, the screen said. *Take shelter.*

I thought of Simon, nervous in his bed when the thunder came booming. And Adrienne, my wife, alone in bed. Our bed. Adrienne and I met back in college, in a bar not unlike this one, during our university's homecoming. When the place got too crowded and noisy, she took my hand to leave, and eighteen years later she still hadn't let go.

I set my glass on the bar and thanked her for the shot. "I think I should go," I said.

"Yeah. Looks like we're in for some rough weather."

"It was nice seeing you again," I said.

"Likewise. Goodnight, Patrie."

"Goodnight."

The sirens were sounding as I left the bar. "Thought you were a better man than this," I said to myself as I opened the car door and slid behind the wheel. Lightning zigzagged across the sky so it looked like cracked glass. I tried to remember how much I'd had to drink. Told myself I was okay to drive.

The kitchen light was on when I got home. Adrienne was still up pouring herself a glass of water. "Can't sleep?" I asked, locking the side door behind me and stepping toward her. She just looked at me. "I'm sorry," I said.

She set her glass on the counter. Her face was bereft of emotion. It was all channeled into her voice. "What's going on with you?" she asked.

"It's nothing."

She crossed her arms. "Please don't do that."

"Do what?" I asked.

"Pretend like I don't know you. You acted like a jerk before."

I was ashamed of my behavior, and yet I felt compelled to try and justify myself. "I feel adrift." It was a weak response, barely even an excuse, but it was all I could come up with to convey how I'd been feeling.

Silence. The refrigerator droned.

"Adrift from me?" Adrienne asked.

"No," I said, recalling the image of her taking me by the hand so many years ago and pulling me back from the edge tonight. "You're my anchor."

A small exhale escaped her mouth. "Adrift how?"

"As a son," I said. I hesitated then, thinking of Simon one floor above. "As a parent."

Adrienne approached me finally, touching my arm. She was thinking of Simon, too. "I need a partner in this, Andy." I closed my eyes and nodded at her. "It's late. We'll talk about this more in the morning. Catch the light on your way up."

I attempted to be quiet coming up the stairs, but the landing creaked under my feet, and I heard Simon ask, "Where were you, Dad?"

I peered into his unlit room, the lightning outside silhouetting pillows, stuffed animals, and him somewhere in the middle of it all, and said, "Away for a moment. But I'm home now."

"The sirens went off."

"I know. We'll be okay. Try and get some sleep."

Lying in bed, with the wind breaking over our home, I remembered how I once got caught: a green and white checkered lawn chair, the storm tumbling in over treetops, slanting gray rain falling fast, thick, and no room between drops. As I ran for home, I couldn't breathe, so low, so dark, those clouds, that sky. I thought of the woman and her red lips amidst that caliginous barroom. I thought of Simon, who believed he was no longer a boy. And I thought of how suddenly, like the forward edge of a weather front, one life could supplant the other.

A PROPOSAL

It was December 1999, a few days before Christmas and several days before Y2K. Americans were wondering if their credit card debt would be erased or if the computers would shut down and send us all into some kind of anarchic squalor. I was on a plane bound for Prague in the Czech Republic. I had never been on a plane before. I had never been outside of the continental United States. And I was heading abroad at a time when most people were uncertain about the future. But I felt distant from all of them. For me, the future was very clear and certain. There was a larger purpose that balanced all of the risk: Adrienne. I was covering such vast space to ask her to be my wife.

The plane jostled within some turbulence. I remember twisting in the small seat, my left knee popping into the aisle, moving like the needle on a sewing machine.

A man, who could have been my father, with the same peppered beard and thick bifocals, asked me, with an Eastern European accent I could not place, if it was my first time.

I looked to my left, at his stout frame barely contained in his aisle seat, and nodded at him.

He chuckled and then, in an act of clumsy reassurance, told

me, "This ... this is nothing. Pray we don't hit any air pockets." He smiled and sipped a rum and Coke. "One time, when I was flying, the plane hit an air pocket. I saw the liquid in my drink shoot straight up out of my glass and come down again, back into the glass. I thought my stomach might do the same."

I nodded at him again and then pulled my headphones from around my shirt collar and searched for the PLAY button on my Walkman. I turned to my right. The man next to me had already fallen asleep sitting upright. I gazed over him, through the oval window, into the black sheet of night thrown over the sky. I was still hours away from setting down in Prague. I had plenty of time to think about how my life had found itself in this direction.

I met Adrienne in the fall of 1997. I was commuting from Eau Claire and student teaching in Rice Lake. She was a senior at the University of Wisconsin, where I would receive my degree. It was homecoming, and we were both a little drunk. We excused ourselves from a crowded, noisy bar. She took my hand as we crossed the street to the trail that followed the Chippewa River. I've already mentioned how she hasn't let go all the years we've been together, but that's not entirely true. In the fall of 1999, she left me for the Czech Republic. It was something she had promised herself a long time ago, she said. She wanted to be truly independent: no family to rely on, no boyfriend influencing her choices. She was going to teach English as a second language in Prague. She was going to hop on a plane, travel thousands of miles across an ocean, and not knowing a single soul, establish a life of her own for twelve months.

"It'll only be a year." She said this as if she were going away for the weekend.

It was a Saturday night. Labor Day weekend. We lay in bed listening to the clang of third-shift metal workers coming from the factory beyond the river behind our rental and to the holler of teenagers in our neighborhood, for whom the night was still young, blow in through our window screen.

The September wind slid over our skin. I shifted under the blankets so my face was inches from hers. "I know this is important to you." I tried to sympathize, but deep down I feared losing her. In two years we had begun to create a life together: running within a social circle, renting the upstairs of a house, watching the moon from a wooden deck above the garage while the people who lived below us argued. But she had always been upfront with me about wanting an experience overseas, someday, on her own. And, although that someday seemed to have come quickly, I knew it wouldn't be right to stand in her way.

"You should come visit me," she said, the thought suddenly occurring to her. "You have two weeks off for Christmas."

By this time I had found employment. I was in my second year teaching high school English at my alma mater. I'd indeed have a winter recess, same as the students.

"Yeah, I should," I said, knowing it was only so much lip service. One of many plans lovers had uttered through the ages that came to naught. Also, Christmas was over three months away. A lot could happen in that time. "What if you meet someone else over there?" I asked. "Some well-traveled European guy, ruggedly handsome, who is into snorkeling and mountain climbing and all this really exciting stuff and—"

Adrienne cut me off. "We'll send you a postcard from the top of the world." She smiled and attempted to tickle my ribs like a xylophone.

I pulled away from her. "I'm serious."

"I know you are," she sighed, "but we've gone over this. We decided the best thing is to break it off romantically. If I meet someone ..." She saw me flinch and added, "Or if you meet someone ..." I rolled my eyes at that prospect. "It'll just be easier if our relationship didn't complicate things two thousand miles away from where we can properly deal with it."

"Damn it," I said, without anger and with some resignation in my voice. "Why do we have to be so rational about this?"

"Because we're saving ourselves from any potential heartache," she said.

"Well, the plan's not working. My heart's already aching."

She moved in closer to me, kissing my chest and then my face. "Do you want to spend my last night in Eau Claire glum?" She looked at me. "Or should we give each other something to carry with us while we're apart?"

We folded into each other and made love in the white streetlight under the tambourine shadows of shaking trees.

The next morning I drove her to her parents' place in West Bend.

On Tuesday, I was back at work. It was back-to-school night for the parents. When I got home, there was a message on the answering machine. Adrienne had called from the airport, her voice punctuated with tears. She said she loved me and missed me, to take care, and that she would call or email as soon as she was settled. *Settled*, I thought. I remember the long, empty hours I waited for that first dawn without her.

True to her word, she wrote immediately and often. She had gone through training and was living with a girl from Texas and a girl from Australia. They were renting a section of a house from a Czech family. She enjoyed the work she was doing and was enamored with the city. The people she had connected with in her program had become fast friends. There was no mention of other men. "You would love it here, Andy," she closed one of her emails.

The next two months became routine, like an exercise regimen.

I taught during the day, I'd email Adrienne, and, some nights, my friends took me out for drinks. At the time, it seemed to help. It's worth noting here this was an era before the ubiquity of cell phones, social media, Skyping, FaceTime, and Zoom calls. Neither Adrienne nor I could afford bloated phone bills, so we were left with email. If there was a misunderstanding across cyberspace, if I misread the tone of something she wrote, for example, given the difference in time zones, it'd often be twenty-four hours before she could respond, and vice versa (which is hard to imagine today in this age of instantaneous text messaging). But there was a general feeling of warmth and love in our exchanges. She still hoped I'd come to visit over Christmas. One night, in an uncharacteristic moment of freakish spontaneity (remember, I was the homebody kid too scared to attend summer camp and the adult who went back to teach at his high school), I decided I'd go. I spent the next day working out the details with her and the airlines.

Closer to Halloween, my friends and I had gone out for dinner and drinks. I decided to tell them about my plan to visit Adrienne in Prague and a newly hatched plot to ask her to marry me. The news took them aback, especially when I explained I didn't yet have a ring. I had, instead, the proposal. Not just any proposal, I assured them, *the* proposal to end all proposals. I reminded them of the song "12 Days of Christmas." I was going to write her twelve poems and give them to her, one at a time, except for the initial six I'd have to provide her with when I arrived on December 19, culminating in an acrostic poem that spelled out WILLYOUMARRYME? It would be a Shakespearean sonnet, fourteen lines long, the number of letters in the question: WILLYOUMARRYME. They expressed concern about the timing; she'd still be in Prague for eight more months after the proposal. Maybe I should wait until she returned home?

CLUMSY LOVE

I did not let the lack of resounding approval on the part of my friends deter me. I spent all of November and part of December, right up until my flight, writing and revising my twelve poems. It was difficult to keep the secret from Adrienne in our regular emails. And I looked for inspiration everywhere. Given my state of mind, it wasn't hard to see signs of "us" in everything. When I pulled into my school's parking lot one overcast morning, I saw two birds in the sky, each seeming to mirror the other's movements, but never touching. *That's us,* I thought. By the end of the day, I'd written a poem about it.

Another time, as I tried to sleep, I could hear a late November rain beginning to turn to snow on the air conditioning unit I'd neglected to bring in for the winter. I wrote a poem entitled "Chrysalis" about how relationships can change states over time and become something ethereal.

I wrote a poem about the various knickknacks she left behind. How the mug she purchased from Caradori Pottery had grown to resemble her: shapely, cerulean blue like her eyes. How, if I held it to my ear, I could hear the ocean or her whisper, synonymous now. And, as I brought the lip of the mug to mine, I was waiting to be taken by her current.

It occurs to me today I was probably spending too much time alone in that rental, but it also made for a frenzied period of inspired writing. I shared work with my colleagues, who I know now shared the same concern as my friends. Looking back, they were less outspoken than my friends, but there was a reticence on their part after reading my work. Rather ambiguous well wishes like, "I wish you all the luck in the world, Andy." I also shared the work with my students. Their "oohs" and "ahhs" gave me the leap-before-looking adolescent encouragement I needed to further justify my single-minded mission. By this time, everyone in my life knew what I was going to do.

But this last thought was of minor significance to me as the captain announced we'd be landing in Prague soon. The plane made the journey without issue. As I debarked, my pace quickened down the accordion umbilical into the terminal. I braced myself: four long months. I stood still, a stone in the middle of a river of people, and could see no trace of Adrienne. My mind raced through the possibilities: she forgot, I told her the wrong date, I'm stranded in a foreign country with no place to go. I decided to sit down and wait. Grumbling, I took out my John Irving novel and began reading.

Ten minutes passed. The people had thinned around me. Adrienne still hadn't shown. My head oscillated from one end of the terminal, as far as my eyes could penetrate, to the other. It dawned on me the error might have been on my part. I hadn't fully exited the terminal. Sheepishly, I gathered my things and followed the *arrows* to complete the last leg of my journey.

I wandered through hallways, past security where they stamped my passport, before stepping out into the public.

"I was beginning to wonder if you got cold feet," a voice said from behind me, for the area was virtually empty.

I turned and, behind a bouquet of flowers, was Adrienne. She wrapped her arms around me, my head crinkling the plastic about the flowers. I returned the embrace. I still remember the feel of the corrugated fabric of her red coat.

"Everyone on your flight came and went," she said into my collar. "I didn't know what to do."

"Stupid me," I said, her blonde hair filtering my words. "I thought you'd be greeting me when I got off the plane."

I could feel her smile slide across my neck. "You've seen too many movies."

We pulled apart just enough to see each other's faces, though our hands held fast to the other.

"You look good," she said.

I tried to make the words work, to express how beautiful she carried herself, as if she and Prague had always known each other. But she didn't let me speak. "Come on, we'll get a taxi."

I gave her half the poems that evening at her flat after meeting her roommates, who gave us plenty of space to be together. She was touched and approved of the work. She said it was a thoughtful Christmas present and couldn't wait to have all twelve. The plan was working as I'd hoped.

The next five days were spent lounging in Adrienne's bedroom at the flat, socializing with her roommates in the kitchen, or exploring Prague. We visited the Charles Bridge, "a place for lovers," she told me, which I took as a sign. We wandered the streets, in and out of various curio shops. We often took cabs into the city and ate every meal out. Adrienne earned a Czech wage, so this was an extravagance for her. But I didn't have to pay for lodging while there, and the dollar exchange was incredible, something like 1,300 for every 100 U.S. dollars. When we did take a bus or the tram, I was careful not to draw attention to myself as an American. Adrienne told me she had heard it said, "No Czech ever smiles on a tram in Prague." Something to do with their history under communism and the dark weight of its memory on their spirits. It sounded apocryphal, yet it was easy to spot other Americans: loud in their laughter. Everyone we passed smoked and checked a cell phone. Adrienne tried to get me to say some of the Czech phrases she'd picked up ("*Dobre den*") and pronounce the streets we passed, like the one that sounded like "*Garaja de vitska*." It was exciting and anonymous, and we were together. I continued giving her one poem a day.

On Christmas night, Adrienne and I retired to her room following dinner with her roommates. I gave her the last poem, not so subtly entitled, "A Proposal." We were on her bed: a mattress on the floor. I watched her lips move as she read, her eyes as they scanned. I was looking for some sign: a twitch in her cheeks, a raising of her eyebrows, something to let me know not only if she understood what the poem was asking but if she was leaning toward a "yes." She had a disappointingly flat affect when she said, "It's nice. You don't normally do rhyming stuff, but it's nice."

"That's all you have to say?"

"Well, yes," she said. "I'm more partial to some of the others, but it's nice."

"I think you need to read it again." She gave me a confused look. "Go on."

She read it again, and again, and again. Her jaw dropped. Precisely the reaction I'd been anticipating. She looked at me, and I smiled back at her. "Are you serious?" she asked. "Are you asking …" Her eyes welled.

"I am." I leaned in closer to her. "Adrienne Walden, will you marry me?"

"I … I don't know … what to say … whew." She fanned her face with the folded poem.

"Usually it's a yes or no," I said. "Hopefully the former."

Suddenly, she embraced me. Almost as hard as when we first saw each other again at the terminal. I returned the embrace. "Is this a yes?" I asked.

"No," she whispered. "No, it's not."

I slowly let myself out of the embrace and stared at her. Was she joking? Had I misheard her?

Sensing the disconnect, she reiterated, "I can't agree to marry you."

"Well …" Inside, I was flailing. "Why not?"

"It's not the right time," Adrienne said.

"What do you mean 'not the right time'?"

"I think you jumped the gun on this, Andy."

"What?" I was losing my cool. "Haven't we had a blast together these past few days?" She nodded. "I think it's pretty clear you still have feelings for me." She nodded again. "We've already lived together. That worked out great. Why not take it to the next logical step?"

"I do feel close to you, Andy," she said. "And I love you." I tried to interrupt, but she put her hand to my mouth. "And I think what you are doing is so very genuine and heartfelt and sweet, but I can't say yes to you."

"Why not?" Whatever anger was present had turned to almost pleading.

"It's not fair of you to ask this of me right now," she said. "I'm in a different place. As you wrote in that first poem, I'm 'half an earth away.' I won't be home for eight more months."

I imagined my friends saying, "Told you so."

Adrienne continued, "This is my time now. I have a life here that's mine. I promised myself to see this through. You knew that, and that's why I can't say yes right now." There was silence and then the sound of snow against the window. I wondered if we had any snow on the ground back home for Christmas. "Andy, how are you right now?" she asked.

We made the most of the time I had left there. My flight back was Tuesday the 29th. I tried not to bring up my overeager misstep, and Adrienne was considerate and affectionate with me. When we said our goodbyes, it was difficult for us to part. There were many tears.

"I can't believe we have to do this again," I said, remembering our last night together back in September, our intent to save each other from "potential heartache."

"I'll write you soon," she said. "Maybe you can come visit over spring break."

"Yeah," I smiled. "Maybe I'll write you some more poems."

"I'd like that." She returned the smile and kissed me, and then it was time for me to go.

I don't remember much of the flight back. There was some turbulence, but it didn't seem to matter that much. I was more concerned with how my family, friends, colleagues, and students were going to react when they converged on me, like the villagers who came for Frankenstein's monster, and asked what happened. How did it go? Did she say yes? I had risked it all for love and had been rejected. Facing my supporters, truthfully and forthrightly, was the least attractive of my options. Instead, I thought maybe I could lie and say I chickened out; I lost my nerve and never gave her the last poem. Or maybe the Y2K bug would mess things up so badly that no one would have the interest or the time to ask me anything. Well, the year 2000 came, and the world didn't dissolve into chaos, and I had a lot of explaining to do.

For the record, Adrienne did move back to Eau Claire. And, once again, she moved back in with me. And as we awoke one rainy morning together, she turned to me and said, "Yes." Sometimes, though, the better story is the one where things don't go as expected.

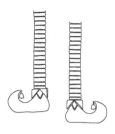

NO GOOD DEED

After Simon was born, whenever he cried, I found it difficult to pacify him. I tried everything. I bounced him in my arms, my lips to his ears, murmuring "shh-shh-shh." Nothing worked. In my desperation, one evening I hissed a "SHHHHHH," which sent his head careening backward in fright and left me feeling horrible. In the morning, I confided to a colleague about what had happened. He was pouring himself a cup of coffee in the teachers' lounge and grinned. "Get used to it, partner," he said. "Plenty more 'father of the year' moments to look forward to." A night out at the bar, nine years later, when I should have been home, certainly counted as one. And six short weeks after that night, in late December 2015, I was on the precipice of yet another.

The snow swirled like smoke across the windshield, creating tiny apparitional vortices. One might call the motion magical in another context. But the snow was starting to accumulate on the interstate, and traffic had reduced to a lumbering roll. The darkness of the solstice had dropped all around us. We could only see our reflections in the window glass and dashboard glow. Under normal driving conditions we would still be a couple hours from Adrienne's parents' place in West Bend, Wisconsin—forty minutes north of Milwaukee. We were eastbound on Interstate 94, near Wisconsin Dells. Who knew how many hours it would be now? With Christmas only a few days away, there was the promise of light's return. For the moment, though, it felt like the longest night of the year, an abyss of darkness and ice. At nine years old, every move Simon made in the back seat grated on my nerves. His iPad was too loud. His Elf on the Shelf, which patrolled the back of my headrest, kept bumping into my head. "Will you put that thing away?" I barked. Adrienne reminded him that Dad needed to concentrate on the road. All three of us had shifted into our default positions for when road trips got harried. In Simon's words, "Dad gets mad. Mom gets stressed. I get annoyed!" And so we collectively agreed to simmer in silence for an indefinite period of time.

It was close to eleven o'clock when we finally pulled into the driveway, tired and tense. I could see the Christmas tree through the bay window alternately blinking red and green. We gathered up our things. I lugged the blue plastic clothes basket overflowing with gifts from the back of the car. My in-laws, Bob and Karen, bleary-eyed from waiting and dozing in front of the television, met us at the front door. They received us with arms around our shoulders, my mother-in-law's kiss upon my cheek. Fox News bleated from the living room, and I counted one of winter's blessings: it was too cold out for Simon's dress. We set down our bags and belongings. I was scurfy with snowfall and stamped my feet, shaking it from my pants to melt into little puddles on their lacquered floor. "Anybody hungry?" Karen asked, her glasses momentarily fogging against the influx of cold. Without waiting for an answer, she moved to the kitchen, opened the refrigerator, and soon produced a buffet of cellophane-wrapped bowls and dishes: cold cuts, cheese, veggies, crackers, chips, and homemade salsa. Adrienne and I looked at each other. We only wanted to slip into bed, but our weariness would have to wait.

"How was the drive?" Bob asked.

I glanced at Simon, who still looked annoyed. "Long," I said.

Although Adrienne and I picked at the spread half-heartedly, it was tough not to be thawed by Bob and Karen's hospitality. Yet as we sat around the kitchen table, we kept the conversation neutral. No word about Simon's visits to the therapist. We asked about the restaurant Adrienne's parents owned. They asked me about teaching. Simon sat to Bob's left, drawing with crayons some scene that would undoubtedly wind up on the fridge. I watched Bob drape an arm over Simon's shoulder and snuggle him close.

We bid Bob and Karen goodnight and carried our things to the basement. We dragged a mattress for Simon from the spare bedroom, past the pool table, and fit it like a Tetris piece flush with the sectional couch where Adrienne and I would sleep. Adrienne threw down a sheet and blankets, and Simon took out his pillow from his bag.

"It smells musty down here," he said.

I rolled my eyes. Adrienne jumped in before I could respond. "You'll be fine," she assured him.

We changed into T-shirts and pajama pants while Simon continued rummaging through his bag. "Don't forget," he said, pulling out his Elf on a Shelf. "Tonight's the night." He stood up with the elf in one hand, iPad in the other. I watched him padding off to the bathroom, excited about Christmas, still a child but one now limned by our worry and sense of upheaval.

"Dad," Simon called. "Come check out my elf."

Each night, while Simon slept, the elf "got up" and reported on Simon's behavior to the North Pole. Simon made sure to note where the elf was in the house before falling asleep. When he awoke, the elf would invariably be in a different spot, clutching an edible treat in its soft hands. Because we were traveling to his grandparents' place for Christmas, we allowed Simon to bring the elf along. He was determined to catch his elf in the act of moving around and procuring that treat. Bob and Karen's bathroom was the one room in the basement where we left the light on all night. Simon figured this was as good a spot as any to film his elf.

I stuck my head in and watched him. He set his iPad on the counter next to the sink, opened it, and used it as a camera to record the stationary elf he placed in front of it. He adjusted the angle so the view captured most of the room, too. "Do you really think your elf wants to be filmed in the bathroom?" I asked. Simon ignored me. I changed the subject. "Do you have enough battery for that?"

He nodded.

"What about disk space, or whatever?"

He sighed, "Yes, Dad."

The exasperation in his voice pushed my buttons. "Listen, buddy—" I began.

Adrienne appeared in the doorway and said, "Let's all just go to bed."

Sometime in the night I woke up to use the toilet. The couch was unforgiving on my lower back and kidneys. The bathroom light reached out to where we lay, so I was able to navigate around Simon's sleeping body without much trouble. The carpet felt coarse beneath my bare feet. When I got to the bathroom, I stopped. The elf's head was twisted sideways, staring at me as if I'd walked in on him doing something he shouldn't. *Creepy elf*, I thought. *Maybe they really do move around at night.* And then another thought presented itself: in order to get to the toilet, I would have to pass in front of the camera. *Kids, and the things we do.* I spread my body flat on the floor and army crawled to the commode. My joints cracked along the way, and I remember hoping the iPad's microphone range was weak. I pulled myself up and then sat down to pee so as not to add the tone of my tinkling to the soundtrack. I thought of Simon, who also sat down when he peed. "Like a girl," he said. As if gender could be so simply determined by the way one urinated. But that was the prevailing wisdom, and bathrooms remained, for the most part, gendered spaces. Adrienne and I were aware of the problems bathrooms posed for trans kids: which one to use, who could see them, and what they would see, but so far Simon hadn't talked much about bathrooms other than to declare his preference for sitting while he peed.

I finished and glanced over at the elf. *Hope you enjoyed the show*, I thought, and then, to my horror, realized I could see myself on the iPad screen. My mind flashed first to ghosts of toilets past: my mortifying hospital stay four years ago. That memory was soon replaced, though, by an image of some future sleepover where Simon and his friends unknowingly uncover this footage of a half-naked father caught on camera in an excretory act. I felt a pulse of rage inside me directed at Simon and his setup. I thought of Dave Seville, admonishing his chipmunks, and could hear my voice screaming, "SIMON!!!" And then I turned that rage toward me and my sleepy brain and admonished myself for not noticing the toilet in the shot earlier. I thought of the car ride down from Eau Claire, my short fuse, and the coagulate snow—an icy menace on the roadways yet still astonishing in the headlights' beam. And it was the season of reflection, of forgiveness, of better days ahead. *What the hell. You want to see the elf move? Let's make him move.*

The top of the elf's tapered hat was out of frame. If I could get ahold of the tip of that hat and yank it quickly enough, it should look as if the elf magically whisked himself away. I approached both elf and iPad, mindful of keeping myself off camera this time. Hovering over them, I formed my right index finger and thumb into a pincher. I thought of the game Operation, the tweezers used to pull the patient's funny bone, the *buzzzzz* if you touched the side. This was the most careful of extractions. I slowly lowered my fingers while keeping an eye on the screen. *Steady, now.* My heart rate quickened. I thought of Simon's face come dawn when he rose to find the elf vanished from the bathroom. *Almost there.* And again, Simon's face when he checked the playback to discover he had recorded a Christmas miracle. *Just a little farther.* I allowed myself a small smile. *Got it.* In the split second it took me to grip the hat and pull, I saw my fingers appear on screen, down to the first knuckle, and then disappear with the elf. *Buzzzzz* sounded in my brain. I overshot my target. I'd botched it.

I leaned against the doorframe and frowned at the elf in my hand. I was at a loss for what to do next. How would I explain this to Simon? I decided the best thing to do was get rid of the footage altogether. I would concoct a tale for Simon, something about how elves, like magicians, did not want their most precious tricks revealed, and so his elf, using a bit of the old elfin magic, prevented himself from being recorded. I didn't feel good about lying. Still, I picked up the iPad, pressed "stop recording," and dragged all incriminating evidence into the "trash." I returned the device to its original position and then stuffed the elf into a corner pocket of the pool table headfirst, naturally, so his plushy red rump could easily be seen. I felt my way back to the couch and immediately fell asleep.

That night I dreamed of stuffed animals suddenly animate and ambulatory, of red tweezers slowly descending. Upon awakening, I felt like something was watching me before I even opened my eyes. It took a moment to separate substance from shadow in the basement gloom. Simon was standing over me. I rose up on my elbows. "Hey, buddy," I cleared my throat. "What's up?" His chest was heaving. "Are you okay?"

Simon glowered at me. "I know what you did," he whispered. I lay back down and sighed. He held up his iPad and played back the footage so I could see my fingers snatching up his elf. I tried to explain, but he walked away from me, past the pool table and the elf's protruding derriere, and up the stairs. It turns out that putting something in the "trash" and *emptying* it are two very different things.

Adrienne, who he had awakened first, leaned over, kissed my head, and said, "Better luck next time, Dad." She got up to follow Simon, leaving me to lie there, blinking in the morning light, thinking about my good intentions, how I was only trying to hide from Simon a world without elves, without Santa, without magic. And creeping in the back of my mind was another truth from which I hoped to keep him hid: Simon's transitioning from boy to girl would mean entering into that tricky bathroom situation and opening himself up to the scorn and judgment of his peers, their parents, and the community. When this scenario unfolds, as it undoubtedly would, I couldn't help but wonder how else I might fail my child.

HIS OR HERS

When dress-up day arrived at Simon's elementary school in the spring of 2016, our third grader woke early. None of the usual cajoling was necessary to shake him loose from his bed sheets. It was a sort of vernal Halloween, a day for students to vent some of the pent-up craziness after enduring a long Wisconsin winter. All around the neighborhood, kids were standing in front of bathroom mirrors preparing themselves, and soon, front doors would burst open to reveal all manner of unicorns, Marvel superheroes, and yellow minions from *Despicable Me*. And then there was Simon, unironically standing before us in the kitchen, wearing a black dress, his pale, skinny arms threaded through the straps. A snarled black wig retrieved from the costume bin in his playroom atop his own mop and flowing over his shoulders. "You sure about this?" Adrienne asked, biting her lower lip. It was the first time he'd worn a dress to school, the first time we'd allowed him to breach that final frontier. Dress-up day was a day where such distinctions were erased, where being odd was commonplace and a kind of camouflage. A boy wearing a dress was, at least in theory, no different from a boy with a horn stuck to his forehead. But, for Simon, the dress was no costume.

Third grade was a pivotal year for Simon in ways other than the dress. He sometimes came home with a wet spot on the crotch of his pants. We didn't think much of it—just a kid too caught up in the responsibilities of the school day to listen to his body. Turns out he was listening but unsure how to respond.

Target stores, whose headquarters were in the Twin Cities, a place many Eau Clairians commuted to, made national news in 2016 with their announcement that "we welcome transgender team members and guests to use the restroom or fitting room facility that corresponds with their gender identity." The world was changing, and being trans in 2016 might not carry the stigmatization it would have even a generation earlier, but the new policy did become a flashpoint for the corporation. There were boycotts. However, other places, like the school district where I teach, would adopt a similar policy the following year, leading to corollary conversations on local media outlets. Overnight, it seemed, all anyone knew about being transgender was that it had to do with bathrooms.

By 2016, Simon no longer felt comfortable using the boys' room at school. He didn't see himself as a boy. He understood others saw him that way, however, and he was a good rule follower at school, so he would just hold it, or try to anyway. He took to wearing oversized sweatshirts that he could pull down as cover and dark-colored pants, hoping any stains might better blend. It was his friend, Talia, who finally forced the issue. Simon told us how Talia, tired of watching him wriggle when sitting and shift from foot to foot while standing, dragged Simon with her into the girls' room.

"How did that feel?" Adrienne asked.

"A relief," he said, and he didn't just mean his bladder.

The incident quickly got around school. Talia exchanged a few blunt words with some fifth graders. We weren't surprised when the principal, Mr. Keeton, reached out for a meeting. I had known Adam Keeton for years and hoped he'd be sympathetic.

It was a Wednesday, and Adrienne and I were buzzed into the building after school. Adam met us at the front desk, and we followed him through the office door and into a meeting room. Large white blinds were drawn across the windows, the gathering sunlight beyond breaking in along the edges. Already seated at the table were Simon's current teacher, Ms. Carson; the gym teacher; the school counselor; the music teacher; and Simon's second-grade teacher, Mrs. Vang. It was a little daunting, seeing all those faces. After all, I was a colleague, a high school English teacher, and I'd sat in on my fair share of parent meetings. But this was a meeting about my kid, and I remember feeling a tiny twinge of shame when Adam phoned, as if my child had done something wrong warranting a call home from the principal. *All this over a place to pee*, I thought. It was more than that, of course, and concerns for his safety were ever present in our minds, yet Adrienne and I would not waver in our defense of him. We took the closest available chairs. Mr. Keeton sat at the opposite end from us nervously clicking his ballpoint pen.

"I want to start," he said, "by thanking Andy and Adrienne for being here this afternoon." He then recapped what had happened in the bathroom. "Whatever we decide here today," he continued, "I want us all to be on the same page." He paused and looked at each of us.

I searched the faces of those assembled for any sign of antagonism. I could hear Adrienne's voice in my head: *We can't keep seeing the worst in people.*

"Finally," he said, "I'd just like to add this isn't about treating

Simon differently. It's about treating Simon with dignity." With that, he set his pen down and asked us how the school could help.

Adrienne and I talked about Simon's coming out to us over the summer. His desire to wear dresses and grow his hair long. His ongoing issue with the bathrooms at school. Mrs. Vang, an early advocate for Simon, whose classroom he did not want to leave at the end of last year, produced a document from a folder, an essay written by Simon we had never seen in which he talked about himself as a girl. "As long as I've known Simon," she said, "this is who he is." The music teacher agreed and shared that one of her siblings had recently transitioned from female to male, adding, "I think it's absolutely crucial Simon be allowed to use the bathroom of his choice."

Stillness. Then, the creak of the gym teacher's chair. *Here it comes*, I thought.

"What about the other students?" the gym teacher asked. "What are we supposed to tell them? That it's okay for boys to use the girls' bathroom?"

"We're talking about one kid," Mrs. Vang said. "And a lot of students already know about Simon. They've grown up with him."

"Tell them nothing," Ms. Carson interjected. "It's none of their business."

"You don't think kids will notice?" the gym teacher asked. "What if some other boy decides *he* wants to use the girls' bathroom, too?"

"We can deal with that situation *if* it happens," Mrs. Vang responded. "Right now, our focus is on Simon."

Adrienne leaned forward and offered an alternative response. "If kids ask, you could always use it as a teachable moment."

I nodded. "Certainly enough misinformation out there as it is." I looked at the gym teacher.

Mr. Keeton placed his elbows on his knees. "How about this," he said, pulling us toward consensus. "I'll make the bathroom in my office available to him as well. That way, if he is feeling awkward about using either the boys' or the girls' room, he has another option."

Adrienne and I ultimately agreed to this offer. I thought of Simon's therapist, her imploring us to allow him some "space to pivot" if necessary. Simon's teachers appeared to approve, offering either a thumbs up or a head nod. Only one shrugged her shoulders in a gesture of "whatever."

If you stop and think about it, public restrooms (or changing rooms or locker rooms) are strange places. Where else in the world are we so aware of the glaring differences (and let's be honest, we're not exactly looking for common ground when we're in the john) between our bodies and the people around us?

They can also be confusing places. In "The Instance of the Letter in the Unconscious or Reason Since Freud," philosopher Jacques Lacan points to bathrooms as an example of how signs often obfuscate what they signify. He presents two identical drawings of doors; above one is a sign for "Gentlemen," above the other, "Ladies." "A train arrives at a station," Lacan writes. "A little boy and a little girl, brother and sister, are seated across from each other in a compartment next to the outside window that provides a view of the station platform buildings going by as the train comes to a stop. 'Look,' says the brother, 'we're at Ladies!'

"'Imbecile!' replies his sister, 'Don't you see we're at Gentlemen.'"[2] The signs are correct, but the message is confusing. Both doors lead to spaces where people use the toilet. Why the need for what Lacan calls "urinary segregation"?

In a 2016 article in *Time*, Maya Rhodan reports that the separation of the sexes in the public bathroom originated in the late 1800s as a result of social anxieties about the presence of women in public spaces. "Social norms," Rhodan writes, "dictated that the home was a woman's place. Even as women entered the workplace ... there was a reluctance to integrate them fully into public life."[3] This led to the founding of gender-segregated reading rooms in libraries, train cars (justified as an effort to protect women in the event of derailment), and, of course, toilets. From the vantage point of the twenty-first century, it seems an archaic and pernicious perspective, and while libraries and train cars are no longer segregated, little has changed with respect to the setup of the lavatory. If nothing else, trans kids are forcing us to rethink these spaces: maybe all bathrooms should have private stalls that go all the way to the floor, and so can be all gendered. Perhaps all bathrooms should be singular, one person at a time.

Like most people, I never thought twice about these things until I had to worry about where Simon would use the restroom. And, most importantly, how other people would treat him once he walked through the door.

"Don't worry, Dad," he'd tell me. "I'll be okay."

Don't worry. Yeah, right.

Of course, the gender binaries don't end at the bathroom door. They're pervasive and manifest in everything from

---

[2] Jacques Lacan, "The Instance of the Letter in the Unconscious or Reason Since Freud" (1966).

[3] Maya Rhodan, "Why Do We Have Men's and Women's Bathrooms Anyway?" *Time*, May 16, 2016, https://time.com/4337761/history-sex-segregated-bathrooms/.

children's toys to adult occupations, from clothing to gestures such as crossing our legs or inspecting our fingernails. Once, while I was reading student essays in the basement, Simon came downstairs to inform me it was time to eat but couldn't leave before asking why I was sitting cross-legged like a girl. "Because it's comfortable," I answered.

I thought of Ralph and Jack in Golding's *Lord of the Flies*, the very book my students had been writing about. After splitting into their respective camps, Ralph ventures to Jack's stronghold seeking compromise. They'd been stranded on an island for some time, and their hair had grown long. Ralph notices how the boys in Jack's tribe have taken to tying back their hair. Ralph is constantly flicking his own hair out of his eyes and admires the utility of these makeshift ponytails. He considers doing the same when he gets back to his camp but dashes the thought after realizing comfort comes at a cost of looking "like a girl."

The morning of dress-up day Adrienne was pacing the kitchen. She was so worried about Simon that she packed another outfit for him in case the dress didn't go as planned. We both made sure to leave work early enough to walk down to the school together and meet Simon upon his dismissal. It was a grand spring day. Fuzzy buds were starting to show on the tree branches. Adrienne and I held hands as we strolled. Yet I felt unsettled, unable to shake the phantom stares I imagined from peers and their parents at "the boy in the dress." Kids were already spilling out onto the playground by the time we reached the chain-link fence. Simon soon emerged from the building, momentarily sunblind. He had taken off the wig. "Too itchy," he would later tell us. He spotted us standing beneath the shade of a basketball hoop and sprinted across the blacktop. His dress whipped and snapped with the motion so that he looked less a boy and more an invention of the wind.

He handed me his backpack, and we began the trek home. Across the street were four boys on bikes who appeared to have not gotten the memo about dress-up day. Buttoned shirts and tight jeans. Fifth graders. Too old or too cool for such frivolity. Kickstands down, they crossed their arms and leaned back on their seats, studying us. "Hey," one of them called out. "Why is that boy wearing a dress?"

Simon glanced at me, not out of embarrassment, as if to say, "Why bother and dignify the question with an answer?" Adrienne caught my eye and mouthed: *let it go*. I thought of how free Simon looked in his dress and knew I couldn't.

I said to the boy, "Look around you." I think he thought I was referring to the menagerie of kids in masquerade now filing onto buses or screaming past us. "Beautiful day like this?" I said, gesturing to the birds wheeling against the lapis blue sky, the budding trees, the warm afternoon sun brightening the homes along the block. "A better question is, why aren't you wearing one?" The boy just shook his head and turned back to his friends.

Adrienne looked at Simon. "Good day?"

"Great day," he said, all smiles.

SIMONE

M ost people grow into their names. Simon never did.

A "Notes" section is included in the classroom edition of *Lord of the Flies*. It is revealed that "Simon," in Hebrew, means "listener." Adrienne and I often laughed about this misnomer while parenting *our* Simon. However, the name was prescient in other ways. For example, in the book, Ralph refers to Simon as "queer," meaning funny, strange, or odd, a word later appropriated by the LGBTQ movement and connoting an identity other than heterosexual.

Simon was also a tragic figure in the novel, something our son liked to point out after I told him where his name came from. We were on a car ride to a park downtown, and Simon said from the back seat, "But, Dad, he dies in the book."

"Well, sure," I said, keeping my eyes on the road. "Don't we all?"

I heard him say, "I guess I should be glad you didn't name me after Piggy."

I didn't think at the time how Simon dying in the book also presaged the notion of the name Simon one day dying and becoming our child's dead name.

CLUMSY LOVE

On a May afternoon in 2016, a month after dress-up day, Adrienne and I were coming inside for a glass of water. We'd been working in the yard. Simon was in the living room doodling in a notebook. He briefly looked up and asked, with such nonchalance, "Can I change my name?" We'd been anticipating a conversation about changing his name since the discovery of his journal and his reference to himself as "Graceful." In that moment, we didn't know how to respond other than to say, "Let's think about that for a bit."

There was a kind of grief attached to it all, from which we did our best to shield Simon. That night, after he had gone to bed, Adrienne and I stood in the living room lamplight and stared at the framed photographs on the wall: our boy at the bottom of a monkey pile of cousins on my parents' leaf-strewn lawn, our boy latched to my back in a family portrait taken the previous winter in some snow-latticed field, our boy, shirtless and bronzed by the sun, in swim trunks at the pool, pretending to be a statue, a fountain of water arcing from his mouth toward the camera. I tried to imagine that face streaked with long hair, damp and dark, and draped over the shoulder straps of a one-piece bathing suit. Along with his name, these pictures would have to be replaced. "We're losing our son," I said. I could feel my eyes welling. Unlike other homes, whose photographs charted a predictable, familiar trajectory through the lives depicted, ours would now separate one life from another.

Adrienne rubbed my back and said, "But we're gaining a daughter." I looked at her, her cheeks damp, both of us trying to smile. We gave up and held each other instead, our bodies sagging before that protean shrine.

In the days to follow, the sadness often manifested at unexpected times. While I was standing in the hallway, during passing time at school one afternoon, my colleague Brian asked how things were going at home with Simon. My mind flashed to the photographs on our wall. I said, "I feel so sheepish talking about this."

He settled against the row of lockers. "Go ahead, man. It's cool."

"We know people who've lost children due to miscarriage," I said. "To disease." I looked at the students filing by. "And I'd never think of equating our situation with theirs. I mean, Simon is a happy, healthy kid." I dropped the volume in my voice. "But I can think of no other word for how I'm feeling than 'mournful.'"

"Then that's how you're feeling," Brian said. "Stop trying to deny it."

I half chuckled, half choked back tears.

Brian put his hand on my shoulder. "Look, I don't pretend to know what this is like for you, but I do know Simon is fortunate to have you and Adrienne in his corner."

The bell rang, and I thanked Brian, and then I attempted to pull myself together for class.

As parents, we could have objected to his desire to shed his name. He was Simon. End of story. He could do what he wanted when he was eighteen and living his own life. So, whose life was he living until then? Nature was full of creatures re-inventing themselves, and humans were no different. In Jhumpa Lahiri's novel *The Namesake*, her main character petitions to have his name changed. Lahiri writes, "European immigrants had their names changed at Ellis Island ... slaves renamed themselves once they were emancipated ... Gerald Ford's name was Leslie Lynch King Jr." Granted, the character is eighteen years old and not transgender, but it doesn't change the fact that "tens of thousands of Americans had their names changed each year." I thought of his fairy wings from years ago and wondered if Simon, my beautiful boy, was molting.

Adrienne and I said nothing, half-hoping the matter would drop, but later that summer Simon again asked if he could change his name. We were back in the living room, watching the Summer Olympics in Rio de Janeiro on television. Simon was sprawled on the floor before us, doodling in that same notebook. "So can I change my name?" he asked. "I'm not a Simon." Adrienne and I felt only slightly more prepared this time.

"Names are important," I said and then considered the power behind being able to name yourself, not leaving it up to your parents or doctors and nurses. I also thought about the fact that I had been named twice myself—once when I was born and again when I was adopted. Although my situation was quite different from Simon's, it suddenly felt like a means of connecting with him. "Did you know I was born with a different name than I have now?"

He raised his face up to me. "Really?" he asked.

"I used to be Kevin," I said.

Simon giggled.

"What's so funny?" I asked.

"Nothing," he laughed, and then he asked, "How come you changed your name? You're not transgender."

I squatted down next to him. "No, I'm not. I'm adopted. Do you know what that means?" Simon shrugged his shoulders. "It means Grandma and Grandpa couldn't have any children of their own."

"How come?" he asked.

"Some people who want to be parents just aren't able to," I said. "And some parents just aren't able to take care of their children, so they give them up for adoption. That's how Grandma and Grandpa found me. My birth mother wasn't able to care for me. I was Kevin then until they adopted me, renamed me Andrew, and raised me as their son." I paused while he took in this information. "What do you think?" I could see him connecting the dots.

"So just because you have kids doesn't mean you're a parent," he said. "And just because you can't have kids doesn't mean you can't be a parent."

"That's right," I nodded.

He then added, "And just because you're born a boy doesn't mean you are one." I stood up and looked at Adrienne. "Dad?" he asked.

"Yeah, buddy."

"If you could name yourself," he asked, "what name would you choose?"

"I think I'd still go with Andrew. How's that sound?"

He smiled. "I like Andrew."

Adrienne stepped in. "And what about you, honey? What name would you choose?"

We crossed our fingers behind our backs hoping he wouldn't say "Graceful."

"I really like the idea of making 'Winter' my middle name," he said, "instead of 'Alexander,' since that's what you were going to name me if I was born a girl."

"And what about your first name?" I asked.

He set down his pencil and mused for a moment. "When Mom and I were at the beach last week," he said, "I told her I felt uncomfortable telling kids I was Simon. She told me to tell them I was Simone. She said it's easy to remember because it's so close to Simon."

Easier for us, for the grandparents, for everybody, I thought. I looked at Adrienne and raised my eyebrows in relief. The name kept the original Simon but also allowed our child to be Simone. Retraining our brains to account for the pronoun changes, to go from he/him to she/her, would be the challenge.

"And what do you think about that?" Adrienne asked.

Simon turned his head toward the TV. It was a moment that, even now as I write this, feels totally scripted. And yet, it is true. There, on the TV before us, was American gymnast Simone Biles receiving a gold medal for her performance at the Olympics. Her name filled the bottom of the screen while she beamed and accepted the accolade. The fact she was a Black athlete in a predominantly white sport wasn't lost on Simon. He'd always been most aware of those who pushed against the status quo. "Simone," he said. "I like Simone."

We revealed her new name in a series of deliberate steps. That August, before her fourth-grade year, we gathered family and friends at Lake Altoona Park for a naming ceremony. We hadn't gone to court yet. But we felt it was important to share her name with our friends before we asked for the legal system to stamp its approval.

We rented a pavilion fringed by slender pines. Red needles and green lichen covered the shingles. The structure was within running distance of the playground for the kids and walking distance of the bathrooms for the adults. There was a view of the lake, its surface silvery in the early evening sun, like fish scales. We arrived early to plug in our crockpots and lug out our coolers. Adrienne staged balloons and ran a banner across the archway. I pulled a picnic table flush with one of the pavilion's stone pillars and leaned a cork poster board against it. I examined the various artifacts tacked to it, including the poem I'd written for her when she was five, titled with her now-dead name. It read:

ANDREW PATRIE

Sometimes I think whenever awakened by
the plastic bite of vampire teeth
or the trailing tickle of a dress
which fits like you were never strangers
that you are not wholly of this earth
rather delivered by moonlight
which first filled your crib like hunger

You move always with the force of autumn
an explosion of light and color in your wake
littered leaves spread upon the living room floor
your world rendered on 8 ½ by 11 pages
where a "grave riser" scratches at the air
your mother is the sun
and you the princess come to lift the curse

Sometimes I worry about you
as I know all too well
the school yard code against
those who lack the "playground blood"
the surreptitious glares of others
I hope you will remain strong in the face
of those who will try and shake you loose

Tell them your roots were never of this place
and dance like the moon unmoored
its reflection rippling
across a river's surface
my son,
how can this world so heartened
not seem less heavy

Reading it now, I thought of how our lives had always been funneling toward this moment: the emergence of "Simone."

We spied Ari and Rachel tramping through the grass, a salad bowl in their arms and Gita carrying a large, wrapped present. Then colleagues from work arrived, former students, Adrienne's college roommates, all thronged beneath the vaulted ceiling. Those with children watched them scatter like marbles to the swings and slides. My sister, Nikki, her husband, Jim, and my nephews sent their regrets in a text message that included the following imperative: "YOU GO SIMONE!!" Adrienne's parents, Bob and Karen, made the four-hour trip up from West Bend to be there.

My parents were the last to arrive. Ironic given that they lived in town. They'd had a front-row seat to the myriad changes in our family. My dad's feelings on the subject were a mystery. My mother, who had spent most of her time every pre-school Wednesday with Simon, seemed to get it: the dresses, the dolls, the drawings, all the ways children turn out to be strangers to their parents. More so than the average kid, my adoption baked in a sense I was somehow different from my mom and dad. I knew Simone felt the same way. Although biologically she was our child, she was not made in the cisgender (a person whose sense of personal identity and gender corresponds with their birth sex) image of her parents or her immediate family and friends. This naming ceremony was an opportunity to help her feel more like herself, less like a stranger.

I went to greet my parents as they pulled into a parking space. They had insisted on bringing the cake, so their tardiness made me a little nervous. My mother was in the passenger seat, her window down, the sun a fierce yellow dot reflecting in the left corner lens of her glasses. "Thought you both forgot," I said, half-jokingly. Then, I saw the white hospital bracelet loosely encircling her right wrist and internally berated myself. It was I who forgot, in the haste of our preparation, that she had said they'd pick up the cake after an appointment for her monthly cancer shot. "I'm sorry," I said, opening her door and helping her to her feet. "Everything okay?"

"Everything's fine," she smiled. "We can talk about it later."

Everything wasn't fine. No transformation (i.e. Simone's happy naming day) is ever happening in isolation from other transformations. My mother was beginning to have trouble with her mobility and digestion, and it would all come to an end three summers from now. In that moment, though, with the distraction of the day's event, it was possible to both see and not see these changes and thus believe my mother was, indeed, "fine."

My dad raised the hatch of his Equinox and began pulling out the sheet cake. He was clad in a red ball cap, faded gray T-shirt, and khaki shorts, his legs impossibly hairy, even at seventy-two. My legs had remained patchy since puberty three decades ago, and yet, I noted how easy it was, in this man's presence, to feel like that insecure teenager all over again. I remembered getting lippy with my father once (well, more than once) in high school and those hairy legs giving chase half a block through our neighborhood before he tackled me onto the Thompsons' boulevard. Breathless, I'm not sure either of us knew what was supposed to happen next, but with our hearts hammering and my eyes bugging out of my skull like some cartoon, I had gained a new appreciation for the man. Most of this newfound appreciation came as a result of our height differential. I was six feet three inches, almost a foot taller than him, and thin as the grass into which his ample Budweiser belly had pressed me. But those stumpy legs were pistons that propelled him at a speed set to break the sound barrier, or maybe that was only my shriek of surprise as I lay in a heap beneath him.

I shook off the memory and went to his side. Standing next to him, I could see his socks were mismatched. It reminded me of the way some high school girls wore them. "Looking trendy, Dad," I joked. He looked at me. "Your socks," I said. He looked down, grunted, and then returned to the cake. I thought I caught his eyes lingering over the red cursive icing that spelled "Simone." I offered to carry it for him.

"I got it. I got it," he said, and then he paused. "Where is ..." His gaze tracked right for a moment to a couple fiddling with their boat trailer and then returned. "... she?" he asked.

I smiled and hoped he could read in it my gratitude. I knew, on some level, he was struggling with all this, but he still showed up today, doing the right thing, carrying that cake for Simone. "She is somewhere near the swings." He nodded. I closed the hatch and watched him walk the cake to a vacant picnic table.

"You know," my mom said, startling me. I thought she'd already moved on. "It's about time we had a granddaughter in this family."

It was this comment that sustained me for the nearly three hours we had the pavilion. And after the crockpots were emptied, and the coolers were more ice than aluminum cans, it was time to call Simone to the center of our small crowd. We were able to pry her loose from her play with the promise of dessert. Adrienne and I both said a few words, thanking people for coming, for their love and understanding, and then we all raised a toast: "Welcome, Simone!" She focused on her feet poking out from beneath her dress, muttered a thank you, and then turned to the cake.

"Are you ready?" Adrienne asked, and Simone stuck out her tongue and panted like a dog.

Everyone laughed and someone shouted, "Somebody get that girl a piece of cake!"

The following spring we had our day in court.

After filing paperwork with the clerk of courts, we had to publish on three separate occasions in our local newspaper that a court date was pending for a name change: "Simon Alexander Patrie" to "Simone Winter Patrie." Public notice was part of the process to ensure all parties were aware of what was happening. However, the paper got it wrong and published "Simon Alexander Patrie" changed to "Simon Alexander Patrie." We didn't catch this until there wasn't enough time to fix it before our scheduled appearance. Adrienne had to file paperwork again for a different date; this time the paper got it right.

The morning we were to appear before the judge, we were a mass of nervous energy in our rush to make it out the door on time. Simone was in her room in a black-and-white polka-dotted dress, brushing her hair and, as our lawyer friend Rachel had advised, practicing her line, "Your Honor." Adrienne and I were downstairs in the living room before the wall of family photographs, and she was helping fit my tie around my neck. "Seriously, Andy," she said. "You're forty-two years old, and you still can't tie a tie."

I winced as she pulled it tight against my Adam's apple. "But I'd miss your loving touch."

I tracked Simone's thudding footfalls down the stairs, and soon she was standing beside us. Adrienne adjusted my tie one final time. Simone was looking at the old photos of herself. I knew what they meant to Adrienne and me. I wondered what they meant to her.

We stepped outside. I was pleased to note it felt like sweatshirt weather again. Blue sky. Warm sun. The last of winter lay in a receding gray line along that portion of lawn still enshadowed under our home's overhanging eaves. I could hear the melt running through the iron grate at the end of the curb. Anonymous birdsong.

The Eau Claire County Courthouse was a stark contrast: a monolithic building three stories tall, neutral colored brick and a row of windows at the top shaped like jail cell bars. Our courtroom was in session, so we sat in the cushioned chairs and waited. That the cushions were the same orange as the correctional jumpsuits was not lost on me. Aside from a week's worth of jury duty, I had never been before a judge. As a kid, I remember accompanying my father to the Chippewa County Courthouse on weekends, about a twenty-minute drive from our home, when he needed to go in and get some work done. He worked in data processing for Chippewa County. His office was in the same building as the courthouse, and he'd sometimes let me roam an empty courtroom. I would look up at the bench. Judgment always came from above: God, the gavel, my father's graying eyes. Every guilty secret I carried seemed to rise to the surface and overwhelm me. I looked over at Simone. If she was at all worried, I was unable to discern it in her body language: back straight, eyes ahead, hands folded in her lap.

The courtroom door opened. The people involved in the previous case departed, and we were escorted inside. Other than the three of us, there was only the judge, the bailiff, and the stenographer. We took our seats and were instructed to speak into the microphones. The judge was quick and clinical, though unable to resist letting slip a little smile whenever Simone leaned forward to address him as "Your Honor."

"It's my understanding you wish to change your name from Simon Alexander Patrie to Simone Winter Patrie?" he said.

"Yes, Your Honor," she replied.

"And you do so under no duress?"

"No, Your Honor."

He looked at Adrienne and me and asked, "Mom? Dad? Is it your wish this child's name be changed from Simon Alexander Patrie to Simone Winter Patrie?"

We both replied separately, "It is, Your Honor."

"Since all parties are in agreement, I see no reason why it shouldn't be so." He struck his gavel. "Best wishes to you, Simone. Court is adjourned."

I followed Adrienne and Simone out of the courtroom, back through the building, and to the front entrance. Before heading outside, I looked down at Simone and said, "Well, it's official. How do you feel?"

"I wasn't sure about that 'duress' part."

Adrienne gave her a gentle side-hug and said, "You did great, sweetheart."

We wanted to celebrate. The week after Simone's court date we booked a room in a hotel with a pool so she could swim. Simone was excited. We bought her a new one-piece bathing suit for the occasion. It was black with dashes of color running down each side like a rainbow of ribs.

Simone had been growing her hair out. Adrienne was helping her put it in a ponytail in front of the living room mirror. I opened my wallet and produced a driver's license, my first, twenty-seven years gone, plastic laminate starting to separate from the photo caught in the amber of its yellowing. The picture was still visible: me with a mullet falling well below my shoulders. I held it up so Simone could see. "What do you think?"

"Gross, Dad," she said.

I placed the license behind the most recent one in my wallet and slipped it in my pocket. At sixteen I never once thought of my long hair as something feminine. It was about social rebellion. Never mind I looked like every other dude into heavy metal music at the time. At least I didn't look like the athletes in my high school. Or my parents. For Simone, though, her hair was both a feminine marker and a means of rebellion. I smiled at this commonality between us.

Adrienne finished Simone's ponytail and said, "Why don't you go put on your swimsuit so you'll be all ready when we get to the pool."

Simone looked at her reflection in the mirror, at that thick faucet of hair flowing out the back of her head. Then her dress twirled as she strode gracefully from the living room. I wanted to share her confidence.

The last time we swam at a hotel was for her ninth birthday party. She'd melted down, in a very public way, over not being able to wear a dress. Granted, things were different now. She was "Simon" then, but, as Simone, beyond a small circle of family and friends, she'd yet to really be out in the world. I remember thinking: *Will people accept her as she is, not as she was?*

"Ready, Andy?" Adrienne called from the kitchen.

I grabbed the green duffel bag, and we made our way to the car.

We stopped for lunch at Simone's favorite restaurant on our way to the hotel. The server distributed menus. With page after page of options, these menus were the length of a short novel. When our server returned, she took Adrienne's order first, then mine, and then looked at Simone and asked, "And what will she be having?"

Simone politely replied, "Chicken dumpling soup," before taking a sip of water, the condensation from the glass wetting her fingertips and then her napkin, where she added an X next to another X in an attempt at tic-tac-toe.

The server, without hesitation, had addressed Simone as a girl. As she collected our menus, I had to look away, feigning something in my eye.

As soon as we checked into our hotel, Simone beelined for the pool. Adrienne took our bag to the room while I keyed Simone into the humid enclosure. Adrienne joined me, and we reclined on the poolside furniture, watching Simone jump into the deep end and splash in goggles too large for her face and already fogging.

We had the place to ourselves, and then, gradually, other families wandered in. Another girl soon waded into the pool, joining Simone, and then a third followed. While those parents could relax their attention and chat or drink or lounge, their children suitably occupied, Adrienne and I pressed our bodies forward, uncertain witnesses, watching the three girls standing equidistant from one another, an awkward, bobbing triangle. Like the server at the restaurant, this felt like another, even more important, test. Would these girls accept Simone as one of them? A few words were spoken between them, and then, one by one, they got out and jumped back in, separately first, then together. We watched as they swam to the shallow end. Watched, too, as one girl interlocked her fingers, extending her arms away from her body to form a makeshift swing. She invited Simone into that cradle, tipping our daughter back, like a baptism.

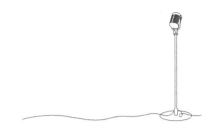

I SING THE BODY TELEKINETIC

It's now early June 2018. Simone is sitting across from us at the dining room table, her plate of food untouched, spinning the dial on her friend Gita's combination lock. At summer's end, Gita will be a seventh grader, a middle school veteran. Simone, on the other hand, is fresh out of elementary school, and summer, for her, is lacking its usual balm. The lock was a gift to help prepare her for sixth grade. She palms it obsessively. It's in her hands more often than her phone. "If you're so nervous about school," Adrienne says, "why don't I call your new principal and set up a meeting?"

Simone pops the metallic arch up, utters a barely audible "Yesss," then snaps it back in place and begins spinning the dial again.

"Simone," I say. She looks up. Her fingers still moving.

"Huh? Oh, sure."

By now, we are no strangers to meetings with school administrators.

A year ago, when Simone's new birth certificate arrived in the mail the summer before fifth grade, Adrienne and I carefully unsealed the envelope and removed the parchment. *Simone Winter Patrie*, it read. I turned to take it upstairs to her room. Adrienne stopped me. "Wait," she said. "I just need a moment." We stood in the hallway and listened to the rise and fall of our breathing, Simone's feet moving over the floorboards above us. "This is monumental," Adrienne said.

"Professor Joseph Campbell says, 'All children need to be twice born,'" I said. He meant first as children and again as adults. Still, I figured the line was also applicable to a kid with two birth certificates.

Adrienne smiled, took my hand in hers, and raised it to her lips.

"You ready?" I asked.

She nodded.

We walked the document up to Simone's room and presented it to her. She set down her sketchbook and accepted her birth certificate, holding it in her hands as if it were a newborn, a wish fulfilled, and any careless handling might unbind the magic.

In order to change Simone's personal information in their computers, the school district required a copy of her birth certificate. This way, when a teacher, for example, accessed Simone's information for attendance or evaluation, the screen would no longer read "Simon." That afternoon we stopped by the district administrative office downtown to make the necessary revisions. We also notified Simone's elementary school. Mr. Keeton requested a meeting with us and Simone's teachers and counselor to discuss the name change, the use of she/her pronouns, and any other concerns. It helped ease the transition into fifth grade that fall for all, especially Simone. When she came home at the end of that first day, she couldn't stop talking about the way her peers had accommodated her.

That was a good experience, but now, watching her fidget

with that lock at the table, we wonder about the next first day in a brand-new school.

Adrienne finishes her dinner and leaves a voicemail to make an appointment with the middle school principal.

The day of our appointment, students are finished for the school year, but teachers are still wrapping up: shuttling textbooks back to the media center for storage, checking in laptops, finalizing semester grades. I know well the chaos we're walking into, what it means that the principal has agreed to meet with us at this time. She is standing outside her office in a trim, gray pantsuit, though all Simone seems to notice are her funky triangle earrings. She introduces herself as "Principal Z." We follow her and the earrings into a meeting room, pull aside some chairs flanking a rectangular table, and sit down.

"Seems weird to be talking about school after just breaking for summer, doesn't it?" Principal Z asks. Simone nods. "Well, I just want to say how very excited I am to know you will be in our building this fall."

"Thank you," Simone says.

"And now I want to know what are you most looking forward to as a middle schooler?"

"Singing in the choir," Simone says without hesitation.

Suddenly I'm thinking about Mr. Frederick, one of the junior high guidance counselors from my youth, a stocky guy with a military crew cut and tinted glasses that lent a brassy shade to his eyes, calling me into his office to discuss music electives. Unlike Simone, I couldn't sing. The only experience I'd had with an instrument was the recorder in fifth grade. I briefly entertained the idea I might be a drummer until I found out I'd have to take a test to determine which instrument best aligned with my aptitude. *With my luck*, I thought, *I'll be matched with a tuba*. This left only one option: general music. "Or as I like to call it, general mucus," Mr. Frederick guffawed. It was a class strictly focused on music appreciation. *Perfect*, I thought. *I appreciate music*. My bedroom walls were a shrine to the heavy metal group Iron Maiden. I queried Mr. Frederick further. He wrinkled his nose as if suddenly smelling something acrid.

"You don't wanna be in that class, son," he said. When I pressed him on why, he replied, "It's full of troublemakers. Miscreants. Your basic anti-social types." His brassy eyes gave me the once-over. "No one you'd want to mingle with. Trust me." It sounded like the perfect place for an adopted, ill-begotten son like me.

I shrug off the memory and look at Simone, thinking here, at least, is one aspect of middle school she won't be brooding over.

"So you're a singer, Simone," Principal Z says. "That's awesome. You're gonna love our choir teacher, Mr. K."

Simone shoots me a look as if to say, *Is everybody around here referred to by the initial of their last name?*

"And what are you most worried about?" Principal Z asks.

"Opening my locker."

Adrienne clarifies, "Simone has been practicing night and day on a lock her friend gave her."

Principal Z is impressed. "Sounds like that's not going to be an issue for you at all. What else has got you worried?"

"Gym class," Simone says before adding, "and showering." It has been a month since our trip to the PATH Clinic in Madison to meet with the endocrinologist about puberty blockers for Simone. And it will be at least a year before she can begin the procedure.

"You know what?" Principal Z says. "Every sixth grader who walks through these doors is worried about that exact thing."

She gets up from her chair. "Here. Come with me."

This is going smoothly, I think. *Too smoothly? Is she dissembling? Does she know I teach in the district? Is that why she's so considerate with our child?* I push these thoughts aside, though. I recognize it's my nature to suspect dark motives in others when it comes to Simone, yet I try to heed Adrienne's advice: to not always expect the worst from people. Instead, I shift my brain and focus on how grateful I am for Principal Z's efforts today.

We follow her through a set of double doors, past the gymnasium on our right, to the entrance of the girls' locker room. We all peek in. Benches sit bare, and rows of red lockers hang open, their undone padlocks suspending in the air. Several bathroom stalls. I can see the teachers' offices at the far end. And waiting somewhere, just out of sight, are the showers. And for the second time since our arrival, I am overcome by memory.

I recall showering as a group in seventh grade, changing out of our clothes in front of our peers, our bodies exposing a diverse pubertal map. All the while, our gym teacher, who was nicknamed "Tex," yet was no bigger than a hobbit, sauntered up and down the rows and told us, in his Southern drawl, "Everyone gets in the shower. Come on now, boys."

I watch Simone take in the layout of the room and think of how these spaces have always been unnerving, and I'm someone whose gender identity is a match with my biological characteristics.

Principal Z picks up on this and says, "Many girls change in a private stall, Simone. And there is no expectation that you have to shower. It's not quite how your parents, or I for that matter, remember it being."

"2018," Adrienne says. "Progress."

Principal Z encourages us to reach out if we have any more questions and wishes us a happy summer. On our way out of the building I ask Simone how she is feeling about middle school.

"Overwhelmed."

"Yeah," I say. "A lot to think about. A lot of unknowns."

"But nice of Principal Z to clear some of them up, anyway," Adrienne reassures.

"I guess," Simone says. "The unknowns are scary."

"Can be," I say. I find myself thinking about that general music class again. I did sign up for it. And, in one sense, Mr. Frederick was right: I walked into a room full of anti-social types. But only if your definition of "social" is limited to playing a team sport. It was mostly boys. In one corner a huddle of four in black Guns N' Roses T-shirts, scraggly hair, and the outlines of mustaches yet to fully form. A group of skater kids congregated in the middle, constantly flipping their sandy bangs from their faces. There were isolates, like me, who did not yet have any allegiance. I took a seat next to a kid with a mohawk. It made him look like some kind of prehistoric beast. I was a bit intimidated, but then he broke the ice. He said his name was Chad. Thirty-three years later, he's still my best friend.

I smile at this thought and say, "Can be pretty cool, too."

The visit with Principal Z may have mitigated such unknowns as locker combinations and locker rooms, but Simone expresses to us she is also worried about meeting new people and the potential for bullying. Following the naming ceremony two years earlier, the whole world did not show up in support of our daughter and her decision. I recall dropping Simone off for a birthday sleepover at a friend's house in elementary school. As Adrienne and I were walking away, we overheard the husband say to his wife, "And what am I supposed to call it? Shim?"

I stopped, turned back toward the house, and steamed up the walkway until Adrienne grabbed my arm and spun me around. "Not here," she said. "Not now." For the most part, though, Simone weathered the transition with little to no bullying. However, middle school might have sharper edges.

It's two months into sixth grade when we hear about an incident.

The yellow school bus stops across the street from our house. The hydraulics settle with a flatulent *pfffttt*, and then the driver levers the door, and Simone steps out. Night is already advancing into the late afternoon. Daylight savings time is nearly finished. I'm home from work earlier than usual and watch her through the window as she crosses the road into our yard, passing under the elm tree. Looking at its denuded branches, I think of how sometimes nature is a bully.

"Dad?" Simone calls as she opens the side door and drops her brick of a backpack on the kitchen floor.

"In the living room," I say.

I hear the cupboard door squeak, the tinkling of glass, and then the faucet gushing. Her hand furrows the leftover Halloween candy dish. I make room for her to take a seat next to me on the couch, but she chooses the chair opposite me instead.

"So it's like that, huh?" I ask.

"What?" she barks. Like the winter chill present in the autumn wind outside, the teenager she will soon become is keen in her voice.

I change the subject.

"Did you bring your music home so you can practice tonight?" Her first choir concert is days away.

"Dad, I can't think about practice right now." She munches a candy corn and then takes a drink of water. "I'm too preoccupied."

"Is everything okay?"

"I wish I had superpowers."

I look at her in her leggings and sweatshirt and appraise her superhero costume. "You know," I say, "we might have to work on your look first."

"Dad," she moans, and I know she is sincere, and so I ease my foot off the playful pedal.

"Okay, okay. Any superpower in particular?"

"Telekinesis," she says. "Like Carrie."

Surfing YouTube, she'd recently come across clips from the 2013 remake of the Brian De Palma film from the seventies based on the novel by Stephen King. She was immediately taken with the character, especially Carrie's ability to move objects with her mind, the character's plight with the bullies, and her final, vengeful fury. The supernatural, be it in the form of religion or telekinesis, has an allure for those who feel powerless. Not so different from the allure of heavy metal music when I was a teenager.

As an incoming sophomore, I was worried about high school and, like most everyone else, developed a kind of defense, a survival strategy, to navigate those halls with minimal harrowing. I grew my hair out and donned all manner of frightening, potentially offensive, heavy metal T-shirts. Before heading out to my grandparents' place to deliver copies of my newly printed class pictures, I remember my mom taking a black Sharpie to them and coloring in the tiny white skulls that were legion on the black shirt I wore that day for the photographer. But my favorite shirt was my Obituary tee; on the front was their band name shaped out of serrated knife blades, and, on the back, in green, oozing letters, the words "Slowly We Rot." It was essentially a "Keep Away" sign draped over my body.

"Did something happen today?" I ask.

Something had.

Simone says, "A boy on the bus told me I can say I'm a girl all I want, but I still have a penis."

"I see."

She twists her glass of water into the arm of the chair. It leaves a dark, wet circle when she lifts the glass to her lips. Still looking at her, I think, *What makes her such a threat?* In an essay I'd read by Judith Butler back in the queer theory class I took in grad school, she talked about a boy murdered by three other boys because he walked with a feminine "swish." Andrew Solomon writes, "Threats to gender are threats to the social order." And I can't bring myself to tell Simone about the lengths some will go to maintain that order. It's still my job to guard her childhood as long as I can. I come back to *Carrie* instead.

"Remember, though, how we talked about what happened to Carrie?" I ask. "How, in order for her to get back at the bullies, Carrie had to become a monster?"

Simone's face creases, as if she is in pain, and her right palm upturns, her fingers drawing in until they resemble claws, as if she is attempting to levitate me off the couch with her mind. "Dad, you just don't understand about the bus!"

Not exactly, I agree, though I'd had my own run-in with bullies on the bus. I tell her about an experience I had in elementary school with the older kids who rode at the back of the bus and cussed and talked about bands like AC/DC whose patches covered their denim jackets like obscene Boy Scout badges. One kid caught me looking and asked me if I knew what they called a girl's privates. "A vajonna," he said, and his friends snickered or punched him in the arm. One of them told him to "leave the kid be." I said he was just messing with me. No way was it called that. More laughter and insistence. My stop was coming up, so I rose and moved down the aisle, their voices in my ears like nettles. When I got to the front of the bus, I wheeled around for the last word: "A girl's privates is not called a vajonna!" The door opened, and the bus lady's blonde head cocked so that one dangling earring skimmed her left shoulder. She turned to me then, her mouth working a piece of chewing gum, and I said to her, "Right?"

When I finish, Simone is smiling a little and asks, "Why are people so obsessed with body parts?" She waits a moment before adding, "Why are people so mean?"

Again, I think of the queer theory class. "Do you know the phrase 'binary thinking'?"

She shakes her head.

"It's a type of thinking that sees things as either or. One or the other. Like black or white. Good or evil."

"Like gay or straight?" she says.

"Exactly," I say. "Or like male or female." I try and explain how the world makes sense this way to some people. Life is either this or it's that, and they can go about the business of living without having to think too deeply about it. But then someone like Simone comes along. Someone who doesn't fit on either end of the binary. Someone who is somewhere in between. Someone whose existence supports the notion that life is more complex than a mere reduction to A or B. And that is unsettling to some people. Perhaps because it reveals something about themselves: *Is it possible I could be queer, too?*

"Are you saying it's my fault the kid on the bus said those things to me?"

"No. The problem is with him. He needs to work through his own insecurity, rather than project it onto you." I pause before asking, "What did you say in response to the kid on the bus?"

Simone looks at a spot somewhere on the floor and says, "I told him at least I don't have a micropenis and then asked if I could get him some hummus for his baby carrot." It's a line from the 2018 movie *Love, Simon*, one of Simone's favorite films, about a closeted gay teen who's being blackmailed by someone threatening to out him at school.

Apparently, Simone does not suffer fools on public transportation, and though I am happy she could assert herself in this situation, I also worry about the potential escalation of such retorts. I want to advise her in case of future confrontations. I think of an essay by Deborah Tannen that I teach in my AP classes, "There is No Unmarked Woman," within which she cites the work of linguist Ralph Fasold who says "two X chromosomes make a female, [and] two Y chromosomes make nothing ... the Y chromosome doesn't 'mean' anything unless ... attached to ... an X chromosome ... [He] points out that girls are born with fully female bodies, while boys are born with modified female bodies."

I say to Simone, "If this boy says anything to you about this again, and you feel you have to respond, maybe just point out to him we all start out as female anyway, so what's the big deal?"

Simone gives me the "huh?" look.

"Why do you think boys have nipples?" I ask.

She repeats the word like "Knee-pulls."

And I say, "Va-john-a."

Our laughter is a small mercy.

Hearing Simone's laugh in the context of that painful moment reminds me how humor can be a kind of superpower, too. When Simone was four years old, my Grandma Catherine, the last of my living grandparents, died. (Technically, Simone was "Simon" then. Subsequent to her name change, however, Adrienne and I also began referring to her as Simone when referencing a memory from the past, from when she was "Simon." It helped secure her new name in our minds and ensured we used the correct pronouns. Going forward, I will do the same in this narrative.) We all piled into the car and followed my parents north on Highway 53 to Bloomer, Wisconsin. It was a cold January night—the time of year when the dark descends over the landscape before dinnertime, and your breath remains visible in the dashboard light until your car has had time to warm.

We pulled into the funeral home lot and parked near my parents. Simone was solemn in the back car seat despite never really getting to know my maternal grandmother. Catherine's health and memory were spotty those last years of her life. I got out and opened Simone's door, scooped her up, and traversed the snow-packed drive with her bum seated on the bend of my elbow and her arms encircling my neck, mittenless fingers seeking warmth beneath its nape.

The yellow glow of the covered lamps inside abated the chill. But Simone did not want to be set down. A room full of strangers, many of whom I did not know, and she hid her face against my own. My parents lingered in the vestibule while Adrienne signed our names in the guest book. We found a row of open chairs. Adrienne helped me out of my coat, Simone still clinging to me.

Eventually, Simone allowed herself a turn to take in the room. People were praying while others sat quietly in reflection. Her eyes were drawn to the open casket. Catherine's face looked waxen yet calm, hands in repose across her chest. I noticed Simone's gaze beginning to track higher to the large wooden crucifix suspended three feet above the casket. Simone inhaled sharply. "Dad," she cried. "Look!" She extended her right arm and pointed at the cross. "It's the protective necklace!" Her voice filled the room. "Now, she'll be safe from the vampires." There were a couple gasps and looks our way, but also quite a few smiles. Adrienne blushed and busied herself with her purse. I choked down a laugh, tried to shift Simone's attention, and made a mental note to never again show Simone the movie *Vampire Circus* the night before a wake. But, for a brief spell, we all forgot we were mourning.

Humor has saved me in my professional life as well. Every year for Christmas my sister gets me a daily calendar. Past themes have included zombies, unusual words, and frightening facts. But the perennial favorite is the "Dad Jokes" calendar. I keep it on my desk at school and use it to defuse contentious discussions. The days rip past one five-by-five square pun at a time. Like this one: "I was accused of being a plagiarist. Their words, not mine." In the pin-drop silence that immediately follows my recitation of the day's pun, students are distracted from their quarreling and, once again, unified in a collective disdain for and amusement with their teacher. Thus restoring balance to the universe.

Whether it's the somber confines of a funeral home or the pressure cooker of a high school classroom, humor is a shield able to deflect the arrows of time and circumstance. The trick lies in knowing when the moment is right to wield it. I am not always the most percipient reader of those moments.

During our drive to Madison last May to consult about puberty blockers, and despite Simone's best efforts to project a cool exterior, I knew she was deeply anxious. Some part of my brain, awake to the unspoken tension in the vehicle, began ransacking my memory files and withdrew a folder entitled "Forgotten ephemera of the 1980s ... recall with caution." It managed to slink past my prefrontal cortex, like a spy smuggling documents by a dozing security guard, and started rifling through the pages until something struck it as humorous and clever. I looked at Adrienne, who was driving, and said, "We're goin' on this trip to see Simone's doctor, yeah, and get her some blue blockers, uh!" I pulled my arms across my chest. It was a parody of the rapper who appeared in the eighties commercial imploring audiences to "get ya some" BluBlocker sunglasses.

Adrienne stared at me, baffled.

"Don't you remember that sunglasses commercial from when we were kids? BluBlockers?"

"So?"

"That's what they're going to do to Simone."

Adrienne asked the next question slowly, as if she was a psychologist worried about her patient's perception of objective reality. "They're going to put sunglasses on Simone?"

"No," I laughed. "They're going to block," I put the next words in air quotes, "the blue," before adding, "as in boys are blue; girls are pink."

The joke flatlined.

"Here, let me cue up the clip," I said, reaching into my pocket for my phone.

"Dad, stop," Simone said from the back seat. Her irritation intensified. "If you have to explain what the joke means, it isn't funny."

Sometimes it's worse when they do get the joke.

One Christmas morning, Simone was on the living room floor tearing into her presents, and Adrienne and I were on the couch watching her. Wrapping paper took flight as Simone uncovered

CLUMSY LOVE

her most coveted item: a signature Woody doll from the *Toy Story* franchise. I waited until Adrienne sipped her coffee, leaned in, and said, "Funny, I got you a signature woody for Christmas, too."

Adrienne almost spit out her coffee. Her eyes widened, and she covered her mouth with her hand. She swallowed and said, "Hope you kept the receipt."

After our conversation about the bus bully, I leave Simone to prep for her choir concert a scant forty-eight hours from now. She takes a break to say hello to Adrienne, now home from work, and another to sit with us for dinner. I watch her as she eats: the tightness of her jaw, the indentation of her brow. She is still perturbed by the day's events. Later in the evening she seeks solace in her electronic devices. A little screen time to stave off reality. She is sitting in the living room when I walk in to check on her. I should probably leave her alone, but something compels me to try and break the tension. It is the same part of me that conceived the "blue blockers" pun, which delights in student groans as I read jokes from a daily desk calendar.

I say to her, "You're on that thing so much, I think I'm going to start calling you Si-phone instead of Si-mone." It's a throwaway line, definitely not my best work. She drops her phone to the floor and curls into a ball in her chair. Now I've done it. Adrienne is eavesdropping from the other room, shaking her head at me. All I want is to foster within Simone the idea that humor can be a kind of talisman against all that assails us in this world. Just like that "protective necklace" she believed was keeping my grandmother safe from vampires. But that lesson, it seems, has been quashed by yet another of my ham-fisted deliveries.

"Hey," I say, bending down closer to her ear, the top of her lobe peeking out of her hair. "I was just trying to be funny. I know you had a tough day. Forgive me?" There is no response. "How about a high-five?" Nothing. "A fist bump?" Still, nothing. "Middle finger?" Movement. She shifts her body so that one eye peers out at me from within a tangle of hair. Like in that Japanese horror movie, *Ring*, right before the ghost girl kills you. Simone slowly raises her right hand, curls her fingers into a fist, before finally unfurling her ring finger at me in a crude imitation of the rude gesture. It is a perfect "dad" joke.

Two nights after the bus incident we drive to the school for her first sixth-grade choir concert. Rather than call the bus company, Adrienne and I have decided to wait and see how it goes with the bully. We told Simone to pick a different seat far away from him. Per her teacher's instructions, we drop her off at school a couple hours before the event. She waves goodbye to us and then enters through a door with a white number "1" above it. If she's at all anxious, she doesn't show it. Adrienne and I fill the downtime by driving aimlessly around town. We stop at a Kwik Trip for gas and snacks. Adrienne picks out a rose to give to Simone after the show. When we return to the school, the parking lot is packed. We pull into the first open spot we find and then hurry inside the building.

The middle school auditorium is red row after row of butt-numbing plastic seats affixed to metal bars and equipped with desk arms which can be stored at the side or used to further obstruct traffic as we say "excuse me" and slide past those already seated. We shed our bulky outerwear and cushion our seats with our coats, trying not to elbow the people to our left and right. We are locked into position for the next forty-plus minutes. Forget about crossing your legs. Don't even think about getting up to use the bathroom.

The room dims, and the chatter subsides. Stage lights focus our attention ahead as the sixth-grade choir walks from the wings to designated spots on the risers. The girls wear black dresses; the boys wear white shirts, black pants, and red ties. An older woman sits at a piano on the far right. From somewhere behind us the young teacher comes sprinting down the aisle in a long-sleeved dress shirt belted into his khakis. He leaps onto the waist-high stage in one fluid motion to address his students. "You know," I say to Adrienne, "I used to be able to do that. Bet I still could."

"Shh," she whispers.

He turns to face the audience and requests we keep our phones out of sight, that a DVD of tonight's performance will be made available for a paltry sum if we wish to have a recording. He then mentions the programs in our hands or laps and praises the work ethic of this group of sixth graders. He points out some songs will be sung as a choir with a few solo "spotlight" acts interspersed throughout. Simone is one of the "spotlight" acts. I scan the list and find her name in the concert's midsection. Adrienne and I have time for one nervous glance at each other before our conductor spins a 180, calls the kids together, and the show begins.

My earliest memory of Simone singing is when she was two years old. Adrienne and I were in the parking lot of a TGI Fridays. I was carrying Simone so her face looked over my right shoulder at the couple behind us. Out of nowhere she belted out a verse from a popular Katy Perry song of the day: "Hot and Cold." It was in the broken cadence of a toddler but still quite intelligible: "You chain your mine like a gurl chain-nes close; yeah, you P-M-S like a beetch I would know." The couple tried stifling their laughter while we, mortified, fumbled our way through an apology.

The singing did improve with time, but what remained constant was both her fascination with pop music, particularly female singers, and her impulsive need to belt out whatever tune happened to be stuck in her head, be it in the car, in the middle of the night, or in public spaces like restaurants, retail stores, and restrooms. Once, while we waited for Simone to finish using the restroom, her voice became audible throughout the entire diner as she sang her heart out from inside the bathroom stall. A woman who exited before Simone finished noticed our red faces and commented, "That girl was born to sing."

And so she was. There were many elementary school talent shows where Simone offered her rendition of "Let It Go" from Disney's *Frozen* and the Pentatonix version of "Hallelujah." Unlike sports, where she recognized her own limitations and sought the advice of more athletically gifted kids, Simone's confidence never wavered when it came to singing. She never shied away from a crowd or the spotlight's rapturous beam. And she worked hard at it behind the scenes. But that was in a neighborhood school, with kids who'd grown up around the transition from "Simon" to Simone. This is sixth grade. Students from several other schools commingle in hallways and classrooms. The worry is real. Her bedroom door is often closed now when she practices. There is the occasional thud of something heavy thrown in vexation.

The first "spotlight" act appears three songs into the program: a trio of girls who begin in harmony before the pressure becomes too much for one of them. She stops singing and starts shaking like a hypothermia victim. By the time the tears come, her partners have moved to either side of her in a cocoon of friendship, a kind of buffer against all our eyes. How could they know our gaze is flush with sympathy? When the number ends, the room resounds with cheering and clapping, and we hope these warm vibrations find and sustain her as the trio vacates the stage for the next performance. As I watch them exit, I think what a brave thing it is to face your audience.

The full choir returns for three more songs, and then it's time for the next spotlight act. Simone's up. She stands before a silent audience, her right hand clutching the microphone stand, composed, waiting for her teacher to cue up the music for Shannon Purser's "Sunflower," karaoke-style. No matter how many times I listen to her perform, this is the moment, the lead up to the song, in which my heart experiences a familiar tachycardia, my left leg pounding. It's more than ordinary parental jitters; it's a visceral fear *for her* rather than for her performance. I can't help looking around at the people sitting near me, wondering what they know about Simone. Should she falter, will they extend the same support as they have the other acts this evening? I think, too, of the bully. He's not here, but he's nevertheless in the back of my mind, like a grimacing menace at the back of the bus. I imagine Simone targeted in the stage lights like a prisoner spotted by the guard tower, and I imagine someone standing up and yelling, "Fraud!" while the audience suddenly produces rotten heads of lettuce and tomatoes from their clothing and hurls them at our daughter. And then the piano's sweet melody comes through the house speakers, and Simone's voice is lilting above it, and all else is forgotten.

It's the chorus, rather a portion of the chorus, which catches in my throat: "I'm a sunflower, a little funny. If I were a rose, maybe you'd want me. If I could, I'd change overnight. I'd turn into something you'd like. But I'm a sunflower, a little funny." And I realize she's not singing for an audience—or for me, or her mother, or anyone else in this expansive room—but for herself. For her very existence. And all the longing and the pain buried therein reaches us in notes as precise and poignant as the sound of a shovel striking the earth, and in their excavation, they become as much a part of the room as the ribbon of velvet stage curtain before us, the mosaic of ceiling lights above us, the very breath within us.

The song finishes, and the room seems to exhale before the applause, the whistling, the calls from the audience. No momentary basking, Simone does her usual demurring and shuffles offstage for the next performer. I feel my phone vibrate in my pocket and will later find text messages from friends in attendance, who we did not initially see in our effort to find seating, sharing their approval. My heart rate slows. My left leg stops bouncing. I allow myself another look around the auditorium and note the reactions of strangers visibly affected. I think back to the conversation with Simone a couple days earlier, about superpowers, about moving objects with her mind, like a sudden night wind against the house, invisible yet present in the glass's groaning, like the stirrings deep within which fill the heart and the head and give rise to a voice able to move an audience, if only for a spell. What need for leaping walls within a single bound when you can simply break them down?

VISITING HOURS

The nights Simone can't sleep, she sometimes sings to herself, as softly as one can sing in a house that has gathered itself under the quiet darkness. If Adrienne's awake, she'll check in on her. Or if I'm pulling myself up the stairs from a late-night writing session in the basement, I will sit with her on the edge of her bed like my dad did with me. I didn't see my dad much during the day. If I did, talk typically centered on whatever handyman project had his attention or, depending on the season, how his favorite baseball, football, or basketball team was doing. I had zero interest in engaging with him on these topics, which furthered my feelings of alienation and reminded me I was the adopted kid. So I looked forward to those brief moments at night, at my bedside, when I could chat with him about my day.

With Simone, it's usually some nightmare that's bothering her, which she won't want to discuss. And so she and I will listen to the house creak and crack. Maybe I'll rub her feet through the blankets. While I wait for her eyes to lid down, I wonder if her bad dreams are at all like mine were at her age: childish fears of critters in the basement and devil dogs loosed upon the neighborhood. Yet the dream I dreaded most at twelve years old was the one in which I would see my dad in the distance and, despite all my efforts, could not get to him. He would remain so many steps ahead of me, out of my reach. In my waking life, I felt a part of my family: we sat at the dinner table for meals, traveled to the mall together, but the biologic disconnect of adoption often manifested in my dreams. I'd find myself outside my home, some force compelling me to walk down the hill where I'd see my dad standing before a clotted Highway 53. Cars blurring before him and his tan jacket ruffling in the breeze. His hair, not yet graying, black and thick, like his mother's, capped with a hat that said, "Wisconsin, Land of Cow Pies and Beer Farts." Always he seemed oblivious to the danger. I'd call out to him, hoping he'd turn and look at me. Instead, he'd take a step, and his form was quickly erased by the streak of traffic. He was not struck by any one vehicle. Rather he simply moved through them like a thing phantasmagorical. And for all my longing, I could not follow. I awoke feeling chilled and lonely, got dressed, and waited for the thaw of day.

Early dark. It is the winter of Simone's sixth-grade year. We pull into the drive of my childhood home. "Surprised Dad hasn't shoveled," I say.

"I'm not," Adrienne says. "It's freezing out."

"When has that ever stopped him?"

We rouse Simone from the back seat before exiting the car, crunch our way through snow, clomp our feet at the threshold, and pass through the front door of my parents' split-level.

Mom greets us from the top of the landing. She is thinner from the cancer, yet she seems steady, radiating warmth at the sight of us. Adrienne goes for a hug. Dad is absent and does not appear at the sound of our voices. Simone descends to the basement and its closet of riches: toys, crayons, games. "Hi, kiddo," my mother calls after her.

"Hi," she replies and then only the thud-step of her footfalls.

Dad does not rise to greet his granddaughter, a swirl of activity now that she is free of the car, the cold and her winter clothes. He is seated before the TV in his recliner, lost in baggy blue sweatpants and a T-shirt one size too large, the splayed pages of a newspaper at his feet, on the table next to him dusty peanut shells splintered in a bowl near the remote.

She hesitates as if she has mistakenly stumbled into the den of some hibernating animal.

It's tempting to attribute his reluctance to rise to his still processing the change from "Simon" to Simone. A hypothesis seemingly confirmed when he says, "Now, Simon, don't come running down here and make a lot of noise. I'm trying to watch TV. Go on upstairs if you wanna raise a racket."

We have only just settled into chairs around the kitchen table when thud-step, thud-step. "Mom! Dad! Grandpa yelled at me."

"What happened?" Adrienne asks.

"He told me to go away," she cries, "and he called me Simon."

Like the unshoveled driveway, this behavior, too, is out of character for my father. He is beloved among the grandkids. At a moment's notice, he is usually ready to indulge in some gentle rough-housing, stuff ten-dollar bills into their jean pockets, or give chase with his false teeth protruding from his mouth like a linebacker's mouth guard.

"Why don't you go play in the living room?" I say. "We'll be in here, and no one will bother you."

"But all the good stuff is downstairs," she says.

"Grandpa doesn't want you down there right now," Adrienne says.

Simone pauses. "Is that why he dead-named me?"

I feel a knee-jerk need to defend him because of his age, because of who he is, and I say, "Cut your grandpa some slack. It's easy to forget sometimes."

Simone stares me down. "Is it ... Kevin?" I deflate. She takes her phone from her pocket and heads to the living room.

I wait until she is out of earshot. I narrow my eyes at my mother. "Dad sure knows how to make people feel welcome."

"He's forgetting things," Mom says, looking at her hands, "misremembering things more often."

"Like common courtesy?" I ask. I regret this rebuke as soon as it's spoken. Truth is it *is* easy to forget proper names and pronouns. I have lost track of how many times I have referred to Simone as "Simon," especially in the wake of her naming ceremony. There was a decade of "Simon" to surmount then. I remember that spring waiting for Simone to cross the finish line at Girls on the Run, an all-girls running group, when I saw an old friend from high school who asked if I had a daughter in the race. My mouth opened. I hesitated, struggling to come up with the answer, before finally stammering, "It's ... complicated." Though it didn't have to be.

"Like time," my mother says. "Geography."

She says she's had to remind him it has been six years, not days, since he last visited the courthouse where he worked.

"He was driving us home the other week," Mom continues, "and I had to navigate him through the neighborhood where he grew up."

I imagine shadows sliding over the moonlit snowdrifts, childhood streets suddenly foreboding and unfamiliar, like some twisted twilit carnival ride, and my father's eyes welling and red in the glow of the brake lights from the car ahead.

I'm losing both of my parents, I think. My mom is sick with cancer, and dementia is now setting in my dad. I'd seen behavior like this before.

Decades ago, my grandfather did not rise to greet me either. As we entered the living room, I could never pass the candy dish without swiping a mint meltaway for now and later. I took a seat on the couch next to my dad while Grandpa rocked in his chair. I remember trying to reconcile the black and white photo of the young soldier on the wall with the bald head and bespectacled face before me, forced finally to acknowledge us when my dad said, "Hi, Dad."

Grandpa's head turned to us, his eyes attempting to focus their faded light guttering like blue flame glimpsed through fog. "Oh, hi," he said.

"Honey?" Adrienne's voice. The past recedes like breath on a mirror. "Thought we lost you, too."

"Anyway," Mom says, "can you forgive him? He really is so proud of Simone. We both are." Here, again, is my mom worrying about everyone but herself.

"Maybe I should go down and check on him," I say.

Adrienne squeezes my arm, says she'll see how Simone's doing. I rise and move to the steps.

When I was a kid I was afraid of the basement shapes in the dark and the dead silence before the furnace kicked on or Dad's work saw shrieked. My head was filled with my grandfather's stories of varmints and Gila monsters in the crawlspaces. I feel that fear return when faced with the prospect of descending those stairs to see how Dad is doing.

I think, too, of that childhood nightmare where I couldn't get to my dad, that inscrutable barrier between father and son. Of all the things I imagined separating us in this life—my insecurities about adoption, my decisions concerning Simone—

I never thought it would one day be memory somehow keeping us apart.

When I reach the bottom of the stairs, I see him. Suddenly, it is easy to envision myself in that chair three decades from now and Simone stepping down to talk with me. I wonder if this, too, is the dream she won't speak to me about on those sleepless nights when song is drawn from her voice.

I finally move into his line of sight, and he turns to me.

"Hi, Dad," I say.

He looks up at the ceiling and, as if seeing through the plaster to Simone seated in the living room above, says, "I shouldn't have yelled at her like that."

"It's okay, Dad. I do it all the time."

He returns to the football game playing out on the television in front of him. "You know," he says, "you were never much for sports, were you?"

I sit on the couch next to his chair and shake my head. *Of course*, I think, *this fact you can recall without any trouble.*

DRESS REHEARSAL

My mother's decline is swift. In early 2019, there's an undeniable dip in her mobility when we stop by to visit. She's using a walker now. She looks frail, and getting herself up from a seated position is a struggle. For the first time since Rochester, death feels imminent. Still, she tries to hide it as best she can behind a pleasant demeanor. I think of how fast those seven years since her diagnosis have gone, how much has happened in that time. I think, too, of my father's declining memory, of Simone who, by the year's end, will be on puberty blockers, and of what life will be like without my mother. On a late-night stroll through our neighborhood, where the half-moon in the sky curves like a pregnant woman's belly, I tell Adrienne this is too much change all at once. She just squeezes my hand in response.

Come summer, my mom is in the hospital, shaking her head at her cancer treatments, saying, "The way this one works and that one doesn't."

It's just me visiting today. "Let's hear what the doctor has to say, okay?" I say to her across her hospital bed where she reclines, her body propped by pillows.

The tumors in her pancreas are pushing on her bowel, making it difficult for food to pass. But this isn't what got her admitted. The fall on her way to the bathroom at home, and some intercession on our part, did. I can see purple bruising on her lip where she bit through it upon impact with the kitchen floor. There is a tube running through her nose down into her stomach pumping its contents into an IV slung above her right shoulder, which flashes burgundy now that she has finished her popsicle. There has been talk of an ostomy, which she flat-out refuses, leaving the option of a liquid diet for the rest of her life.

I look out the window, watch birds vainly skimming along its flat surface expecting to find a place to land, to find their footing, and having to adjust upon discovering there is nothing. I think of my mother, how independent she had been until one day she was not, and how this is something not easily surrendered.

I shift my eyes from the birds outside back to my mother nodding off in her hospital bed: mouth gaped, skin sunken around her eyes and at her shoulders, cadaverous in the hospital's low lighting, and far from the robust figure she cut in my childhood. She is like an inhabitant of some other dimension now come with tidings of the future, my future, all futures.

The doctor enters and my mother's eyes slowly open.

"How are you feeling?" he asks.

"Better."

"And how's that tube?"

"Fine. I really don't notice it."

"That's good." He turns to me. "Not an easy or pleasant procedure that tube. Wasn't sure how it would go with your mother."

My mother smiles at the thought of her not being able to handle anything. "I'm tough."

"Yes, you are, Judy," he says.

I reach over and rub the top of her wrist: the skin, the bones, everything so thin.

"I think," he continues, "we'll be able to remove the tube later tonight and see how your body handles things. Okay?"

"Yeah."

"Do you have any questions?" he asks.

My mother shakes her head.

I look from her to the doctor. "Actually," I say, "she and I were talking earlier about her cancer treatments." I watch her throw her arms up as if to say, *Apparently my response doesn't count for anything.* "Are the drugs having any effect?"

"Well, her diagnosis was seven years ago. She's still here."

"Yeah," my mother laughs, "and look at me now."

A few days later I return for her discharge. She is in a wheelchair and waiting for me in the lobby. I take over for the hospital attendant and push her through the parking lot, keeping the talk light and repetitious: the weather, Dad, Adrienne, and Simone. I secure her in the back seat of the car, like she is my child on her way home from a doctor's appointment, and then return the wheelchair.

I sneak glances at her in the rearview mirror. And then I'm thinking about that movie from all those years ago, the one my mom busted my friend Pete and me with, *The Texas Chain Saw Massacre*, the scene of that girl going into that house to die, and I suddenly don't want to take this drive. As usual, my mother is on to me.

"What's bothering you?" she asks.

"I'm worried."

"Yeah?"

I picture her falling at home, and she too proud to reach out for help beyond my father's limited assistance. "I'm worried this is going to happen again," I say, "that it's going to keep happening, and unless someone's around to force your hand, you won't do anything about it."

"I'm going to be fine. You're going to be okay."

I grip the wheel more tightly, suddenly seeing life as a series of seconds arranged on a conveyor belt sliding by as quickly as the trees lining the labyrinth of streets we navigate.

"Remember *The Texas Chain Saw Massacre?*" I say.

"Why would you bring that awful movie up now?"

The story of the "forbidden videotape" was told and re-told within my family for years, well after my friend Pete vanished from my life following high school graduation, right up until this moment preceding my mother's death three decades later.

"Because this time you don't get to eject the tape. We play it out to the end, and we talk about the real possibility of you falling in that house again. Except maybe you don't get back up."

She turns her head away, as was her habit with unpleasant things, including horror movies or cancer, and stares out the window, effectively circumventing the conversation, pulling the plug on the machine. In the silence, I'm nakedly aware of my tone, how threatening it rings, and I'm immediately regretful.

"Mom, please?"

"I'm tired," she sighs.

Life is a slasher film, I think. *We're all just waiting to be picked off.* And it occurs to me then that this car ride may be the last time she and I are ever alone again together. My mind races through all the things I want to say: tell her I love her; beg forgiveness for all my trespasses; express gratitude for her unwavering support of her only granddaughter, Simone. Life could've just as easily placed me with a different mom, one unable to let go of the male-female binary, one who thought Adrienne and I were doing all the wrong things for our child, all the time, and let us know about it. What a horror movie *that* would've been. But my mom brought the sheet cake to the naming ceremony. She loved our girl. What a gift. What a loss.

Again, my mother senses my mood. "What's really bothering you?" she asks.

There is a lump in my throat that I try and swallow over. "It's just—" I'm on the verge of choking up. "Of all the babies you could've had, you picked me." My vision starts to blur, so I wipe my shirt sleeve across my eyes. "And I don't think I ever said thank you for that."

I can't look at her, but I hear her say, "You're my son, my boy. The best I could've ever had."

A small sob escapes me. "Now," she says, "please take me home, kiddo."

BIRDS AND BEES

"Dad," Simone says. "What's a female erection?"

It is August, weeks before her seventh-grade year begins, and weeks after my mom died on a Sunday evening, July 28, 2019. We are on an afternoon hike to the library downtown. Simone and I have just left the tree-lined streets of our neighborhood and are taking a shortcut through the Forest Hill Cemetery. My mother isn't buried here. Her ashes are in an urn at home with my father. But it's nice to walk here and contemplate her life just the same until Simone asks this question and takes the wind out of me. *Is this "the sex talk"?* I think. *Is that what this is?* Since the advent of middle school, the "talk" has been looming like the graveyard monuments we are walking by. Funny, too, that in this place of marble memorials to the dead, we seem poised to delve into the mechanics of life.

"Where did you hear about that?" I ask, hoping my voice sounds as casual as this stroll.

"In a book I'm reading."

Given her generation's access to limitless online information, dubious or otherwise, the fact she read it in a book, and then consulted me, strikes me as an innocent, downright antiquated response, and kind of touching. She looks up at me through her parted hair, just a kid clad in a silk-screened purple T-shirt and leggings, awaiting my response.

"I think it might have something to do with the clitoris," I say. I explain how it fills with blood just like the penis does when it becomes erect. She goes quiet for a time.

We pass a small chapel. Wrought iron bars have been welded over the opaque windows. The slap of Simone's flip-flops against her heels echoes between the leaf-cluttered rise to our left and the ivy-festooned chapel wall on our right. And I wonder whatever happened to simply talking about crushes.

I think back to Simone's third-grade year. The three of us were at a parent-teacher conference with Ms. Carson who asked us a question clearly intended as rhetorical: "Anything else you'd like to discuss?" Simone, still "Simon" then, bravely broached the topic of classroom crushes because of a comment Ms. Carson made earlier that week. Ms. Carson had told the class, "Kids your age do not have crushes." It was no secret Simone was infatuated with another boy in class. However, Ms. Carson had summarily dismissed the notion that the kids in her charge could recognize such feelings, let alone act upon them. It was a way for Ms. Carson to simplify her world, and theirs, but it had little to do with reality.

I can recall Michelle, the first girl to keep me awake at night. We were in third grade at Sacred Heart Elementary two years before my parents would pull me from parochial to public school. Her lips were full and flush like the parish coffers. I spent my allowance, two dollars, a princely sum, on candy from a neighborhood grocer, all for her. At recess that day she shoved the chocolate hard against my chest and shook her head. But it is her eyes that stay most with me, like stained glass, both sacral and tragic.

Adrienne tells me Simone dropped the "female erection" question on her in the Dairy Queen drive-thru a couple days later. Right as she was ordering, too. The cashier had a quizzical look on her face as she handed back Adrienne's change.

"Maybe it's time we had 'the talk' with her, Andy."

I think, *Who am I to dole out such information? What do I know about sex apart from the obvious?* I met Adrienne when I was twenty-two years old and still a virgin. The latter was partly due to an innate aversion to risk and partly due to the mullet I had grown throughout high school. It also had a great deal to do with Catholic guilt. Growing up, I was too afraid to touch myself. I thought God, and possibly my deceased relatives, were watching my most private moments. Like in a cliché mystery, I imagined them behind a portrait, hidden in some secret passageway, and no matter which corner of the room I roamed, I could feel their eyes upon me. This also meant I was prone to nocturnal emissions, or "wet dreams," and further embarrassment as I tiptoed past my mother some mornings to bury my profaned underwear deep within the laundry hamper.

My parents weren't eager to have the conversation, either. But I imagine it had less to do with their own misgivings about their knowledge on the subject and more to do with it being a taboo topic within our culture. So my curious friends and I sought answers from other sources. When I was in seventh grade, I took care of the neighbor's three cats for him while he was on vacation. I remember searching the house for them one afternoon and finding a stack of *Playboy* magazines stashed in a closet. I sat on the carpeted floor, thumbing through them until the room grew dark, already so late in the day, and wondering how I was going to explain the delay to my parents.

We had cable TV in our home, and I was aware of a certain scrambled channel where a young boy might glimpse a bit of nudity. Comedian Dante Rusciolelli calls this "Picasso TV. Like when you tune to the Playboy Channel, but you don't get the Playboy Channel. So it's just a breast up here and an eye over there." I crouched in front of the set in the basement to see what I could see until the warning shot of my mother's feet on the floor above panicked me into switching stations. Sort of like my dad suddenly turning to golf when he heard me coming down the stairs at night. With health class still years away, there were so many questions. The only certainty about sex seemed to be, as one of my friends put it, that it involved "a whole lot of anatomy." Scrambled or otherwise.

I don't want Simone to feel like this, leery of her body, and so I agree with Adrienne we should sit down and have "the talk." Adrienne lets me take the lead. The plan is to roll it out in phases. Phase one: I borrow a book from our friend Rachel entitled *It's So Amazing: A Book about Eggs, Sperm, Birth, Babies, and Families*—I saw it on a shelf on one of our visits—and leave it on Simone's bed one afternoon for her to find, read, and come to us with questions. Answering her questions is phase two. We don't get very far.

Simone is in full middle school dramatics mode, thumping down the steps to where we are sitting in the living room and brandishing the book above her head. "What is this?" she demands. Adrienne and I look at each other. Simone answers for us, "This is a kid's book. Do I look like a kid?"

I resist the urge to say, "You look like our kid," because she has a point. The target demographic for the book is seven to ten years of age. Close enough, I figured.

"I'm not in elementary school anymore," she says.

"Your dad thought it might help," Adrienne says.

"Help with what?"

"The sex talk," I say.

"The *what* talk?" Simone asks.

"You've been asking some questions lately," Adrienne says, "and—"

Simone interrupts. "That was just to get a reaction out of you."

"We thought you might be, you know, dropping hints to us you were ready to have a talk," I say.

"A sex talk?" she asks.

We nod.

"With you guys?"

We nod again.

"Gross." Simone tosses the book onto the couch, turns, and thumps back up the stairs to her room. The windows rattle behind us when she closes her door.

I look at Adrienne, throw up my hands. "We tried."

"Did you even look at this book, Andy?" Adrienne picks it up and flips through its pages. "Maybe part of the problem is that Simone doesn't have a cisgender body but a trans one." She hands it to me. "Not sure this book can answer questions about what sex will be like for her. Anatomically or otherwise."

I ignore the book, inwardly acknowledge yet another of my parental blunders, and think, *Who wants to imagine their child's sex life?* It's like imagining my parents' sex life: one of those things I don't want to think about but have to think about anyway.

When I return the book to Rachel, she asks how it went. She smiles as I replay the interaction for her, as if she expected as much. She suggests a class on sex and sexuality that is running every other Thursday night at the Unitarian Universalist Congregation of Eau Claire. It is for kids Simone's age. Gita, Rachel's daughter, is already enrolled. "I know the instructor," Rachel says. "She's really good." I run it by Adrienne. As reluctant as we are to entrust our child and this most intimate of talks to the care of someone else, after all, sex is more than just procreation regardless of one's orientation, we also know it can be healthy for parents to remove themselves from certain situations, to let others take the wheel. Or the handlebars. I remember trying to teach Simone how to ride a bike on the hill next to the cemetery. On that summer morning, the hill overgrown and green, she was teetering, adamant I not relinquish my grip on the bike. I told her falling was part of learning. I could feel our frustration levels rising like mercury in a thermometer. Rachel's partner Ari and Gita had stopped by to encourage Simone, and Ari offered to try, stepping in so I could cool down, and behold, Simone held her balance a little bit longer and managed to make it a few more feet before gravity made a heap of her and the bike. And I remembered how it wasn't my father but a neighbor lady who finally taught me how to ride a bike. Sometimes, as parents, we can be too close, and we need to understand we don't have to be the wise ones when it comes to every last topic. As Adrienne and I puzzle over how to guide Simone into a world that may not always be welcoming, this class may be an opportunity to hand over some of that responsibility to others.

Adrienne volunteers to pick Simone up from the sex class that first Thursday night while I wait at home wondering how it all went. Simone was actually excited to go, especially when she learned Gita would be there. The evening sun has gone down. The lawn looks like a cluster of blue shadow pools. Soon headlights sweep across the living room walls, dragging a reflection of the window frame with them. The screen door on the side of the house opens, and Simone's voice is audible from the kitchen: "They passed out condoms to us, Mom, and we had to practice unrolling them over wooden penises." There is a pause. "The class was strange but pretty cool. The teacher talked a lot and about trans people, too. She let us ask a ton of questions."

I head into the kitchen as Simone keeps talking. The class, it seems, has helped resolve some of those questions Adrienne and I cannot answer about our daughter and sex. Within its walls, Simone can think openly about a sexual life and without the embarrassment of her parents being present.

Think of our lives as airwaves and sex as the most pirated of signals. For too many of us, though, that signal is warped, not easy to discern, like me attempting to read something in the static interference of the Playboy Channel all those years ago. What a relief to hear Simone communicating so candidly with us. To know that the picture has already begun to unscramble for her.

ESCAPE ROOMS

It was not the first impression I was hoping to make. On our first date, Adrienne and I strolled past Third and Lake, and she asked to see my place. I remember holding her hand and hoping we could keep walking as far as that warm October night would allow. But she persisted. As I reluctantly turned the key to my one-room efficiency, I warned her not to be swayed by what lay beyond. Pay no heed to the movie posters: *Texas Chain Saw Massacre*, *Last House on the Left*, *Creepshow 2*. Or the monster model kits atop the bookshelf. Or the entire Three Stooges collection on nine six-hour VHS tapes. The French doors opened, and she followed me in. We sat on the couch that unfolded into a bed but remained a couch, and we continued holding hands, though we did not kiss because that would have been presumptuous. We remained planted on that bed/couch and talked through the witching hour. I could feel myself already falling in love with her. I remember telling her the blue before dawn was the blue of her eyes. When that first birdsong startled her to rise, I wondered when, or if, she'd call.

And, as a parent, I often wondered when, or if, Simone's friends would give her a call.

Ever since she became Simone, our biggest fear was the acceptance of her peers, not just those she would come to work alongside in various extracurricular activities, but those social friendships that extend beyond a team event or concert performance and are so critical to our development when we are young. We worried she would be stuck alone at home while kids her age gathered at the mall or at basement sleepovers. And so I'd try prodding her into action. Over our long summer together before seventh grade, and while Adrienne was at work, a common conversation between Simone and me went something like this:

"Dad, I'm bored," she'd say, prostrate on the couch, her nose practically touching her phone.

Articles abound on the value of boredom, of switching off screens and doing our own imagining, of adhering to that parental dismissive to "figure it out." I'd suggest riding a bike or asking someone to interact by physically meeting up. But there also exists a wide gulf between theory and practice.

Simone would glance up at me and say, in a querulous voice, "Bikes? This isn't the eighties." She'd hold her phone toward me. "*This* is how kids hang out today." She'd return to her screen and mutter, "Besides, everyone's always busy, and I don't feel like dealing with rejection."

Who does? I'd think.

It is now September of her seventh-grade year, and Simone is turning thirteen. It's our family's first milestone without my mother, or perhaps *millstone* is more accurate. On top of wondering how I will ever get along without a mother, I'm also wondering how I will ever parent a teenage daughter. Simone wants to celebrate by inviting some friends to experience an escape room at the mall, followed by pizza and cake at our place. This creates a momentary panic on our end, as Simone hasn't ever had any of her middle school friends over. We worry about the remnants of "Simon" yet recognizable amidst the collage of family photos on our living room wall. To what extent are we allowed to hold onto our memories of a son who is now our daughter? What is the right thing to do? There is no transgender guidebook for us to consult. Following the name change we added pictures of Simone, in her long hair and dresses, to the wall. Older photos had to be removed to make room. It was a difficult afternoon deciding what should stay and what should go. Adrienne said it felt like we were recording over the past, like on a mixtape where what was originally imprinted continues to softly speak in the silence between songs. Even as we strived to do right by way of the politics of trans issues, we still struggled with our own selfish hearts. We left one family portrait of us, as we'd been, in the center, the new pictures radiating outward from it. In the end it was up to Simone to give final approval. She said she liked the symbolism of this arrangement, like drawings in a cave telling the story of who she was, who she'd become, and so it has remained. And so it will remain, at least through this weekend, when she tells us we need not touch anything on the wall. Her friends know she was once "Simon" and are cool with it. "Out of curiosity, though," she says, "what compelled you guys to buzz cut my hair back then?"

We are happy she has connected with other kids but can't help noticing her lengthy bathroom intervals applying makeup or brushing her hair, the extra attention she pays to her outfit this afternoon. While we wait for her a floor below, in the kitchen, I ask Adrienne, "Is this some new teenage thing?"

"Yes, but not in the way you're thinking."

I stare at her.

"She's making herself special for someone," Adrienne says.

Simone had shared with Adrienne she has a crush on one of

her friends meeting us at the mall, thus explaining the extra primping in the bathroom before we leave. I hear Simone's feet on the stairs and refrain from asking a follow-up question.

She is ready to go, so I dig the car keys from my pocket. As we head for the door, the phone rings. We leave the call for the answering machine. It's Adrienne's parents, Bob and Karen, with an a capella rendition of "Happy Birthday." I don't know it yet, but this will be the last time I ever hear Bob's voice. A month from now we will receive a different kind of phone call summoning us to a hospital bedside where a nurse will take him off a ventilator, and we will say goodbye. In this moment, though, his voice sounds resonant, his lungs robust, no sign of his congestive heart failure over the speaker. Bob once sang for a barbershop quartet, and we smile when Karen slips out of tune with him, and then we close the door.

On the car ride over to the mall, we can't resist pressing Simone for details about this crush. She blushes and tries to shrink herself into her jacket.

"Have you told her?" Adrienne asks.

"No," Simone says.

"Who is it?" I ask.

"I don't want to talk about it."

We pull into the parking lot, running late, and hurry through the café court, weaving through kiosks displaying cell phone cases and T-shirts adorned with the kind of colorful maxims usually reserved for the bumper of one's car. We dodge shoppers riding what look like motorized panda bears and make it to Tactical Escape 101 before the other kids. I check in with the store manager.

We are led to a couch for further instructions when all children are present. One of the girls says, "These cushions look like big, fluffy Cheez-Its." Middle school laughter.

The manager replies, "I think this girl is hungry."

"No," the girl says before affecting the swagger of some YouTube personality they are all obsessed with, "we good."

Simone giggles so hard I think she might pee. I look at Adrienne and mouth the words, *Crush on that one?* Adrienne shrugs her shoulders.

"That's good," the manager says. "Because once we lock you in," she points down a darkened hallway, "the door won't open for a full hour." She has their attention now. "So make sure to go to the bathroom, get a drink, whatever, before we head in. Okay?" The girls nod. "Anybody need to go?" They shake their heads. "The adults tell me it's someone's birthday today." The girls cheer and single out Simone, who grins and looks at her feet. "Well, happy birthday, sweetie. In honor of your special day, we're going to put you in the Conspiracy room. It's my favorite room of all." Eyes widen while I wonder if all the rooms aren't her "favorite." "Let's go check it out."

The seven of us step into the room, the claustrophobic size of a prison cell, while the manager stands in the doorway and highlights the clock we'll be up against, continuously counting down, the camera by which she can see us, and a phone we can call in case of emergency or if we need a clue. She tells us the record times we are to beat, promotes teamwork as the best strategy, and wishes us luck. Then, she closes the door and locks us in. The digital clock begins reversing itself: 60:00 to 59:59 to 59:58 ...

Across from the door is a bookshelf; various tomes with hand-stenciled numbers on the spines are accessible for the girls to grab and scrutinize. In front of us is an old telephone operator's switchboard with its numerous cords and jacks waiting to be plugged into what looks like a giant honeycomb.

"This can't be the entire room," I say.

"I bet there's a secret door," says one of the girls, flipping through the pages of a book. She looks at me. "I've been in escape rooms before."

And she is right.

The numbers along the book spines align with the numbers on the switchboard, and a doorframe hidden within the wall before us opens inward revealing another room. We all cross the threshold, grateful to be leaving this cramped antechamber behind and curious about what new puzzle awaits us.

It is a spacious room. There is a desk along one wall, a mantled fireplace across from it, various maps, and a chair in the farthest corner from the entryway. The manager encouraged the girls to "turn over everything," and they waste no time seeking clues and keys that fit the many locks dangling from desk drawers and the metal box suspended above the fireplace. I am pleased to note that the promised conspiracy angle of the room more fully presents itself here as the girls and their investigating turn over spurious documents related to the 1969 moon landing, John F. Kennedy's assassination, and the Illuminati.

Adrienne and I brush shoulders amidst the chaos and have a moment to exchange a look: *Who do you think the crush is?* Simone hasn't linked up with a single person in the race to beat the clock, now ticking below 30:00, and escape the room. They have divided the labor, each attacking a specific area of the room and calling out to the group when something seemingly significant is discovered.

Soon their efforts open another hidden door in the back wall by the chair. There are cries of delight and affected horror when they step through to find a Poe-esque charnel room littered with plastic skeleton pieces. A seven-foot statue of Bigfoot has been stuffed into a corner, like a botched taxidermy, and is obscured by shadow. Near the entrance is a wooden crate covered with yellow crime scene tape warning the girls, like a pharaoh's curse, to think twice before opening. The lid is off in seconds. Fistfuls of white packing peanuts fill the air. One of the girls retrieves the green alien mannequin within and attempts to dance with it.

I check the clock. "Just under ten minutes."

Watching them bonk each other on the head with femur bones and pretend to kiss skulls they have named after boys in their class, Adrienne says, "I think they're done."

They end up one lock short of escaping the room.

Afterward, they ask for a group photo and if it is okay to use some of the body parts in it. The manager has a spot in the lobby with a small wooden platform, and the girls climb on top of it. One girl drags a disembodied leg up with her, plants the thigh on the ground, and props her elbow on the ball of the foot. A couple girls find some harlequin masks to wear. One holds a sign that says, "I see dead people." Simone carries the lower half of a body with her and lifts the skeletal legs above her ears so as to rest her chin on the pelvis, like a living H.R. Giger sculpture. I snap a photo with my phone, and their laughter is so loud that mall passersby pause what they are doing to look in on us.

The picture gives nothing away as to whom Simone fancies, nor does the rearview mirror on the car ride back to our place. Aside from parental curiosity, it doesn't really matter. The important thing is that Simone has had a happy thirteenth birthday (how far we've come since the waterpark debacle on her ninth). Still, I can't help thinking beyond the moment. Middle school is thirty years behind me, but I remember how fickle those friendships can be. People cool with who you are one day can be using it against you the next. And what about that eventual first date, whether one, five, or ten years from now? I think of that night with Adrienne outside my place, key in the lock, about to open the door to my whole world, the urgent need I felt to confess about who she might find inside. Is that to be Simone's fate as well? Gender politics conspiring to force a confession akin to "by the way, I'm trans" every time she meets someone she is interested in? Or, like with Adrienne, will it simply not matter? When Simone finds herself in that midnight blue light before dawn, perhaps someone will take her hand, cross the threshold, like passing through a hidden door in an escape room, and follow her inside.

ON THE TEAM

My father was an ace bowler and ballplayer. Throughout his forties, I can recall watching him shut out opponent after opponent on the racquetball court from the balcony of the YMCA. Even into his seventies, before dementia set in, his competitive spirit was still readily apparent. The man could play a ruthless game of cricket at the dartboard or Texas Hold'em at the card table, which is why, when I was younger, my father held similar aspirations for me, his only son. Because I was adopted, a genetic mutt, he made it his mission, it seemed, to find the sports gene that must be embedded somewhere within me, in all boys, lying dormant, awaiting only a father's forceful prod. In so doing, a part of him believed our relationship as father and son would have more validity. But athletics and I would never be bedfellows, strange or otherwise, same with band, choir, orchestra, or any other extracurricular camp or club. I craved the quiet space of home to indulge my weird imaginings.

With the exception of her involvement in the children's choir at the Eau Claire Music School a couple blocks from our house, Simone seemed of a similar disposition. That is until middle school. As a seventh grader she signed up for choir and now has added Encore (the middle school equivalent of show choir) and volleyball to her repertoire. Adrienne and I suddenly find ourselves having to rearrange our schedules to ferry her to practices and competitions. Thus, we have joined the chorus of parents this fall who lament the new impositions on their time.

I'm seated on the living room couch, midway through evaluating my first student essay, when Simone approaches me and asks if I'll throw the volleyball to her. I look up to see she is wearing athletic shorts and her team jersey, her hair in a ponytail, and she is staring out the window at the father across the street slinging a football into the eager hands of his two boys in the day's last light. I can almost hear their laughter through the glass. I want to tell her no. I'm too busy. Can't she see the papers in need of grading sprawled out in front of me? But the sun's angle catches her in a broad stripe of light, and she and the evening are lovely. I set my pen down. "Why not?" I say.

Before her first game, a friend asked if we'd ever been to a middle school volleyball match. "There's really nothing quite like it," he said. "If the ball happens to make it over the net, it's a celebration. So much positivity."

"Nice," I said.

Adrienne and I found our spots on the gym bleachers and settled in next to the other parents. We marveled at the mechanics of both teams' bump-set-hit drills, which somehow managed to defy the laws of physics and move the ball backward, away from the net. Serves, Simone's included, were as likely to roll under the net as they were to ricochet off the ceiling. When one of Simone's practice serves hit the center of the mesh, Adrienne and I applauded. When another of her serves sent the ball spinning toward our faces, we ducked.

Sitting in those stands and watching the game also conjured up other concerns—the familiar slow simmer of worry that accompanied every one of Simone's public performances, be it volleyball, choir, or poolside birthday parties. But especially volleyball. Like bathrooms, competitive sports have been—and largely remain—rigidly gendered domains. And, like bathrooms, the reasons for this separation of the sexes, I have learned, are rooted in fears of the feminine: that female athletes might upstage men at their own game. Trans athletes are yet another complicating factor in sports. Stories of trans athletes playing for teams opposite their biological designation are rare but highly controversial and divisive. In 2017, high school track star Andraya Yearwood, a trans athlete from Connecticut, earned multiple state titles and a squall of contention over whether it was fair. As of this writing, more than thirty states, including Wisconsin, have introduced bills meant to exclude transgender kids from athletics. Trans athletes are a perennial scandal in sports, but only when men transition to women. Why?

One reason is the presence of testosterone, especially if the athlete hasn't begun hormone blockers or other therapies. According to a 2020 study in the *British Journal of Sports Medicine*, at the elite level, trans women demonstrate an edge over cisgendered women up to two years after starting hormone therapy.[4] Some have suggested a longer waiting period before trans women are allowed to compete. A reasonable point, perhaps, except that cisgendered South African sprinter Caster Semenya, who dominated at the 2016 Olympics in Rio, had naturally high testosterone levels. Should she have not been allowed to compete as well? And here was Simone, on the cusp of puberty and the flood of testosterone she wanted to dam, serving a volleyball into the net and jogging back to stand in

---

4 Timothy A. Roberts et al., "Effect of gender affirming hormones on athletic performance in transwomen and transmen: implications for sporting organisations and legislators," *British Journal of Sports Medicine*, (2020), 577.full.pdf.

line behind the other girls. I reminded myself this was, after all, only middle school. Yet I felt torn between watching her and watching the crowd whenever she stepped up to serve. Try as I might to assume positive intent in the hearts of others, every eye on Simone that was not her mother's or mine felt adversarial. But she wanted to play. She *demanded* to play. She was not only accepted on the team but was getting time on the court despite not being a "star" player. What parent wouldn't support her?

I follow Simone into the front yard to work on her bumps and sets, tossing the volleyball back and forth between my hands like a wannabe juggler. The father across the street pulls his arm back, nods at me, and then throws a pass to his boys. I'm reminded of my own father's attempts to get me outdoors, away from whatever book had my attention, to hurl a ball so high we'd momentarily lose sight of it in the wide blue sky. Simone and I move to opposite ends of the lawn. Near the fence line she turns to face me, the sun at her back. I lean against my car parked in the driveway and ask if she's ready. I use my left hand to extend the ball away from my body, take a step forward, and make my right hand into a fist. The ball makes more contact with my wrist than fist and sends a shiver of pain up my arm. "Dang," I say, shaking it out. The ball veers too far left, out of Simone's range. She laughs at my ineptitude and runs after it.

"Dad," she scolds. "You don't know how to do it right."

"I guess not," I say, massaging my wrist.

"Didn't you play volleyball when you were little?" She pauses to appraise me. "Or any sports?" She walks over and picks up the ball from the stump of a tree we had removed a month earlier.

"T-ball," I say, holding my arms before me and gesturing for her to toss the ball back.

"Does that even count?" she asks and then sends the ball my way.

CLUMSY LOVE

"It did to my dad."

My father coached T-ball, so there was never any question about if I was going to play. That summer of my second-grade year I donned the maroon Mariners jersey, a great white shark across the front to make our diminutive frames more minatory, and trudged out onto the baseball diamond in that dusty July heat.

Except I didn't want to be there.

Summer afternoons I much preferred the company of Dracula's vampiric bats to baseball bats, but it was my father's entreating eyes when he said, "Just give it a try. A little physical activity would be good for you." I felt the pressure of a father who didn't want his adopted son to let him down in front of the other parents.

I remember one game. I grudgingly approached the T and grounded a single. My father's prayer answered. "Go, Andy, go." I half-heartedly took a base.

The inning slowly ticked by, and then I was in the outfield.

"Keep your eyes on the ball, Andy," my father called across the arid expanse.

My eyes kept straying toward the parking lot.

There was the crack of aluminum against the ball and something that cracked inside of me as well. I walked off the field, heading to my father's car where my illustrated copy of *Dracula* lay on the passenger seat. There was no thought of my teammates, the opposing team, the fans. My father's eyes followed the ball, and then me, as I shambled by him like one of Dracula's brides, unable to ignore the allure.

Simone moves closer to me, as if halving the distance might somehow make me into a more suitable player. "Just throw it to me granny style," she says, bending her knees and cupping her hands, imitating the motion, assiduously coaching me, as if she is the parent and I the obtuse child.

I copy her instructions, send the ball up high, past the boulevard elm tree's leafiest branches, and watch her brain and body make the split-second calculations and adjustments to determine if she will bump or set as gravity brings ball and bone together.

"That was good, Dad. Let's try it again."

We repeat this action over and over until we can barely see the ball in the deepening dark and Adrienne switches on the porch light. I tuck the ball under my arm and notice we're the only ones left outside.

"It's getting late," I say. "School night."

"One more throw?"

"That depends. Does one more mean one more? Or three more?"

"Maybe three?" she grins.

"Okay."

She makes a celebratory motion with her right arm, like she is pulling down an imaginary lever, and then finds her spot in the yard. I marvel at her tenacity and think, *Here, finally, is a playing field I don't want to walk away from.*

LOVE WINS

Winter has come early. It is November 2, 2019, and there's snow on the ground in West Bend. Still, we resist its incursion by not wearing our jackets as we exit our khaki-colored Toyota Sienna, the same color as my pants. My tie catches in the wind and licks at my face like a tongue. Encumbered with flowers, poster boards checkered with photographs, and a small, wooden urn, we cross the parking lot to the funeral home. It has been a month since my father-in-law, Bob, died, and today is the visitation. In between, there have been many cards and condolences. And Adrienne is worried no one will come, that it will just be us, her niece, and her grieving mother. Simone, clothed in a black-and-white funeral dress, holds her hand.

Inside, scented candles sweeten the warm air. I help the funeral director position the photographs on several easels at the back of the room. There is a table for coffee, Styrofoam cups, and syrup dispensers for flavoring. Adrienne's mom, Karen, opens a Tupperware container of cookies that she baked the night before. Adrienne and her niece arrange the flowers at the front of the room. The urn sits beneath a picture of Bob taken some time in the middle of his life when death was practically inconceivable.

I check on Simone seated in an adjoining room, sketchbook open and coloring furiously, and then take my place at Adrienne's side, as she did for me mere months ago when my mother died. I notice the painting on the wall to my right is of a neighborhood in the evening half-light after a spring storm. The ground is wet, the grass green, and the clouds glow orange as if lit from within. White picket fences. A steeple in the distance. Looking closer, I see people, purposefully faded, like ghosts caught in a loop reliving moments from their lives in perpetuity: a boy flinging a newspaper from the sack slung over the handlebars of his bike, a dog in motion, anticipating the arc of the boy's throw, two girls in white dresses and tights disappearing down the sidewalk. I stare at my hands to see if my own skin is starting to wear thin. When I hear the outside door open and the first visitor arrive, I'm grateful for the distraction.

The man coming inside the door is only a few years older than me. He says Bob was his principal back in 1976 when he was a first grader. An older woman soon follows. She used to work with Bob at that elementary school and tells us mornings always took a little longer to get rolling because he insisted on greeting every kid by name. Karen smiles and says, "That was Bob." The line keeps growing. I can see the relief in Adrienne's face as people from the different eras in his life continue to come and share stories. Bob eventually left education to open a supper club. They are popular in Wisconsin for their fish fry, prime rib, and old-fashioned cocktails made with either brandy or bourbon. His current and former employees begin arriving to pay their respects, as do many of his longtime customers.

Adrienne tilts her head back to me and whispers, "My dad really brought people together, didn't he?"

The afternoon goes on. The tributes continue. I return from the bathroom and grab a cookie from the diminishing pile. The line has dispersed. Pockets of people still mingle, looking at photos, laughing at some private memory. I peek in at Simone and find Adrienne is introducing her to a couple who Adrienne used to work with at the restaurant when she was in high school: Ritchie and Allison. Ritchie is asking about Simone's sketchbook, says their oldest child keeps going through them, one after another. Adrienne says it's the same at our house. I think of how I filled notebook after notebook with my stories as a kid. Ritchie says Simone should meet their son someday, that he's always looking to make new friends. I leave to check on Karen.

She is talking with two other women, so I hang back. Ritchie has followed me and appears beside me. He is a heavyset guy with a salt and pepper crew cut and goatee and wears a charcoal dress shirt. He looks past his athletic prime but could get scrappy if the situation calls. He looks at me with understanding, which doesn't quite register. He says, "I just wanted to let you know how nice it is to talk to people who know what we're going through." For a moment I think he's referring to Bob, but then I think about his meeting Simone.

"I'm sorry," I say. "I joined your conversation with my family already in progress. Do you have a child ... like Simone?"

"Transgender? Yeah. Our daughter is transitioning to a boy."

Before I have time to respond, he goes into a story remarkably similar to our own, though their child, now a senior in high school, did not come out until eighth grade. "Saw something on her social media. Figured we'd better have a talk with her." He then corrects himself: "Him."

"If I could only go back to when he was six years old," he says, "knowing what I know now. I mean, all the signs were there."

Ritchie continues to speak with the fervency of someone who

has been given permission to reveal a long-smoldering secret. I just listen, understanding how important and rare these moments are.

"It wasn't easy to accept at first," he says, "and I made so many mistakes. I'm just trying to do right by my kid."

Adrienne and Allison stick their heads in from the adjoining room. I only now realize that we are the only people in the visitation room, save for the funeral director and his assistant taking down the easels.

Ritchie offers one final anecdote about a convenience store visit, how he was able to recognize in the clerk signs of a person in transition, and how the man in front of him in the checkout line was unutterably rude to the clerk. "The kid had tears in his eyes," he says, "and I was next up at the counter." Ritchie shakes his head, holds up his right fist. "Back in the day, I would've let that guy at the front of the line have it, you know? But that wouldn't help this clerk." He looks in the direction of Bob's urn. "Instead, I said to the kid, 'I want you to take a deep breath, okay? Think of something that makes you happy. Because none of us here are gonna talk to you like that. That guy should've never spoken to you in that way.' I looked at the two or three people behind me in line, who all nodded. The kid sobbed and said, 'That guy was so mean.' And I said, 'That guy was so wrong.' But you know what bothered me more?" Ritchie asks me. "The whole time I kept seeing my child's face in the face of that clerk. I was aware of this kid's situation because of my child's situation." He moves his body closer to mine. "But let's say I didn't have a transgender kid. Would I have said anything?" He then takes a step back, eyes on the floor. "Even worse, could I have been that rude guy?"

The room has been cleared of all Bob's vestiges. The flowers, the photographs, the urn have all been packed back into the

Sienna. We rejoin Adrienne and Allison, collect Simone, and follow Karen and her granddaughter out of the lobby. Ritchie and I agree to find each other on Facebook. We climb into our vehicles and depart.

On the ride back to Karen's house, I think of that painting hanging in the visitation room, our own liminal world in which time gradually grinds us all transparent. I think of this new family suddenly swept into our orbit, of how this was the furthest thing imaginable when I woke up this morning to the cold and the snow and the absent chair at the head of the breakfast table. And I think of Bob caught in his own loop, like that fading paperboy and his dog, forever bringing people together.

As a rule, I try to avoid platitudes like "love wins." They are the empty calories of any discourse: utterly delectable in the moment, ultimately offering little sustenance. Sure, I have accumulated enough anecdotal evidence to justify its usage. I think of people like Ritchie and Allison and their unconditional support for their son. I think, too, of Bob. West Bend is a conservative little burg, and Bob was certainly a man of conservative politics, though I never saw anything but a kind smile and an affectionate hug when it came to Simone. But I am also the advisor for my school's Gender Sexuality Alliance (GSA) group. I reluctantly took on the role, as a straight, cisgender man, when a student asked me to after the former advisor moved away from the district and left the position vacant. It's a student-run club seeking to make the school more hospitable for all kids regardless of sexual orientation or gender identity. The past few years have seen an uptick in students who identify as transgender. According to a recent report from the Centers for Disease Control and Prevention, 2 percent of high school students identify as transgender, and 35 percent of these trans students have attempted suicide.[5] For the most part, these are kids held in abeyance in their own homes, unable to talk to their families about who they are, forced to hide behind misgendered birth names and bodies misshapen by puberty. Amidst their stories full of longing for familial acceptance, not unlike the stories of other teenagers, what good is the bromide, "love wins"?

I think of Jaylin, a student in my seventh-hour English 11 course. On the first day of class I mistook her for a boy. It was Lawrence on the attendance list. When I read the name in front of twenty-five other students, she quickly corrected, "I go by Jaylin." I looked up and saw a kid over six feet tall, a week's worth of facial hair covering her cheeks and chin, a rumpled sweatshirt and jeans, clothing large enough to lose oneself in. I nodded at her, at her courage, and made a note on the seating chart.

Jaylin came to trust me. It was partly through my connection to GSA, but mostly through an aside I shared with her about parenting Simone. In the week leading up to parent-teacher conferences that fall she approached me after class and asked if I might do something for her.

I was sitting at my desk, entering grades into the computer. "What do you need?" I asked.

"I was wondering," she began. "Well, I thought you could talk to my parents for me. Let them know there's nothing wrong with me." Jaylin's parents were unsupportive of her identity. They didn't want to talk about name changes or hormonal therapies.

---

5 Michelle M. Johns et al., "Transgender Identity and Experiences of Violence Victimization, Substance Use, Suicide Risk, and Sexual Risk Behaviors Among High School Students — 19 States and Large Urban School Districts, 2017," Centers for Disease Control and Prevention, (2019), mm6803a3-H.pdf.

I opened my mouth to speak, but Jaylin spoke over me, as if to allow my thoughts more time to ripen into words agreeable to her, to prevent them from spoiling too soon.

"I mean, your daughter is trans, and you're a teacher, and you guys are okay."

"Jaylin, I don't think it would be appropriate for me to contact your parents and discuss your gender." Her face was crestfallen. "Your grades, yes," I said. "I can let them know how you are one of the brightest, most articulate students I have this semester. But I really don't think it's my place to talk with them about your identity."

"I understand."

I had a hard time looking at her. I, her teacher, was incapable of assisting her in a moment of need. She was heading for the door. "Jaylin," I said, "wait." She stopped and turned back. "What's your email address here at school?" I told her I was sending her links to a piece I had written about Simone, which aired on Wisconsin Public Radio, and a subsequent Human Health Report interview I did. "These things are out in the public already. Feel free to share them with your parents. Maybe it'll do some good?"

"Thanks," she said.

I clicked "Send."

Jaylin's parents never came to conferences. And I never heard if my words ever made it to a screen near them.

However, a week after conferences I received an unrelated email from a former student named Tommy. He was newly twenty-one, newly enlisted in the armed services, and he was hoping to catch up over a beer. I had already been asked by a friend to read something that Thursday night at the VFW Post 305, just down the road from where I teach, in honor of Veteran's Day. I was planning to read a poem I wrote in 2002 for my grandfather Patrie who fought in World War II. I suggested to Tommy we meet in the bar afterward.

Tommy was a teacher's dream: funny, outgoing, open to applying to his work whatever concepts we were covering in the creative writing elective I taught. He was an award-winning athlete and, thanks to a father the same age as me, Tommy grew up immersed in the excesses of the 1980s, from the hyperbolic spectacle of professional wrestling to the eye-watering pyrotechnics of heavy metal stage shows. I still have a photo of Tommy and me taken in my classroom on Halloween during his senior year. Both of us, unbeknownst to the other, dressed up as eighties rockers. I found the black wig in Simone's costume bin and put it on. A formidable mane running over my shoulders and down my back; it was the kind of hair I would've sold my soul for in high school. I dug out an old Iron Maiden T-shirt from some tour back in the day to complete the look. Meanwhile, Tommy found his best Jon Bon Jovi wig, Bret "The Hitman" Hart shades, and frosted jean jacket. When we finally saw each other, we stopped laughing long enough to look stern and flash the devil's horns for the camera like we'd just been caught by the paparazzi and could expect to see our mugs on the cover of next month's issue of *Hit Parader*.

When the VFW reading concluded, I left as soon as courtesy allowed and made my way through two corridors that connected the meeting hall to the bar. The smell of stale popcorn was strong, and the room was electric with lights, television sets, and conversation. Most of the stools around the bar were occupied, but Tommy got there early and procured a couple seats in the far-left corner. We hugged, I laid my jacket over the vinyl chair back, and he asked what I was drinking.

I invoked the old Halloween photograph of us and called out his short hair, his military issue cut. He laughed at the memory, and then he talked about the impetus to enlist like his father, grandfather, and great-grandfather before him, all of whom were still alive. "Now that's a photo op," I said. Tommy smiled and drank his beer. "It's good to see you, man."

"You too," he said, and he raised his glass to me.

"Cheers," I said and took a drink.

"There's actually another reason I wanted to see you."

I signaled to the bartender for a bowl of popcorn. "And what's that?" I lifted my glass for another drink.

"To tell you that I'm gay."

I stopped mid-lift and set my glass on the counter.

He added, "And to ask if you already knew that. Like, could you tell back then?"

"No."

"Good," he said. "You know what high school is like."

Tommy talked about his carefully curated deprivation, which fooled us all, even himself for a little while. He was, after all, the gifted athlete and soon to be the courageous cadet. He told me about the cryptic journals he wrote for my class, the dark nights he contemplated ending his life, the relief he felt coming out to his sister and now sitting here with me. I leaned over and hugged him again. "Hey man," I said. "Thanks for telling me. I'm sorry you felt you had to keep this to yourself all these years."

"Thanks, Patrie." We relaxed back into our seats. "Thing is, I always wanted to tell you. I figured you'd understand."

"I do," I said. "And I think it's great you're coming out. Have you told your parents?"

At the mention of his mother and father his eyes slid sideways. "No. To be honest, I'm really nervous, especially about my dad. You know what he's like."

I considered my response. "I do know him. And based on what

I do know, I gotta think that if you tell him ..." I floundered here, grasping at words in my mind. There were two words that stood out like the waving hands of students first to respond in a class discussion, and try as I might to resist calling upon them and scan the room for other options, it was inevitable I return to them: "... love wins."

And it did. Tommy texted me over Thanksgiving to say he'd come out to his parents, and while they were hurt he felt he couldn't come to them sooner, they were glad he eventually did. I sent them back all my love and said we all had much to be thankful for this season. I wondered how things were going over at Jaylin's house.

A year and a half later, graduation was in the air, even if it was still April. I was charged with reading names at the ceremony, a role that became mine indefinitely after I agreed to do it one time. It was a job nobody wanted. And I spent much of my free time, in the weeks leading up to graduation, poring over the list provided to me by Student Services, noting problematic names and seeking out accurate pronunciations. Now, it was true that each student was to present a card to me before I read their name aloud, replete with phonetic breakdowns of their first and last names. Still, there were only seconds between my reading of one and another, and I did not want to leave anything to chance, especially with a packed gymnasium of family members waiting to hear their son or daughter's name respectfully recited. Ironically, I only ever mangled the names of students I knew, never those of the Hmong students in our building or those of Eastern European extraction, which was why I was on a mission to find Jaylin and discuss what to do about her name.

It was also National Day of Silence, and our school's GSA hosted an event every year with the blessing of our school's administrative team. Students voluntarily take a day-long vow of silence to acknowledge the silencing of LGBTQ students. Some place tape over their mouths to thwart any temptation to talk. Some carry pens and notepads to communicate as they move from classroom to classroom. They are instructed to break their silence if required because of curricular demands in a given class, but most teachers are accommodating. Out of our school of 1,400 students, maybe 100 actively participate.

Still, there are always phone calls from misinformed parents, worried about some school-wide conspiracy to convert their kiddos, who elect to keep their children home on this day. This year offered an additional dilemma: a student opposing the Day of Silence took it upon himself to print flyers advertising a "Straight Pride Day" and was placing them on tables and stuffing them into lockers throughout the school. While administration was trying its best to collect them (putting up posters was prohibited unless given the okay by a building principal) and discipline the student, I was preoccupied with locating Jaylin.

I found her in a study hall and called her into the hallway. She was one of those participants who both taped her mouth shut and carried a pen and notepad.

"Question," I said. "When I read your name at graduation, what name do you want me to use?"

She looked at me curiously and then scribbled a response on her notepad. "I have a choice?"

"Of course you do."

She thought for a moment and then wrote down: "I'll have to check with my parents. I'll let you know."

"Okay. Let me know as soon as you can."

On graduation night, I sat at my little table equipped with a microphone, a pen, a box for student name cards, and a bottle of water and surveyed the horizon of shoulders rising blue beneath their gowns and arranged in rows across the gym floor. In the bleachers, along the periphery of my vision, blurred forms, like answers hastily erased, moved to their own idiosyncratic rhythm: bodies restlessly shifting, programs being used as makeshift fans against the heat, hands stifling coughs, babies sounding to hear their elastic voices bounce off the gymnasium walls like rubber balls.

The whole process, from the superintendent's speech to the words from our valedictorians to the performances of our school's band, orchestra, and choir, moved effortlessly, efficiently, and soon it was time to read the names of our graduates. Early on I read the last name of a student I knew well from our interactions in study hall as "Pyke" instead of "Pick." A pocket of the audience groaned, and I tilted toward the microphone to redeem myself: "Pick, that is." Too little, too late. Perhaps I needed to get that one mistake out of my system, for the rest of the evening went smoothly, including when I got to Jaylin. Her family had reached a compromise. I was to read her name as it appeared on her birth certificate but then add: "Or better known as Jaylin." I remember a smattering of cheers, even though the audience had been instructed to withhold any public display of affirmation until the end of the ceremony. She smiled at me and then proceeded up the ramp to take her turn across that stage.

As I watched her receive her diploma and shake the hands of various school board members, I couldn't help wondering about her future. Were there positive portents somewhere in that limited cheering? Would I get an email from her a few years into the future letting me know all was well between her and her family? Would love win? There was little time to ponder such thoughts, though, as the next student was already presenting me her card, and Jaylin had vanished back into the crowd.

PSA ON BEHALF OF GSA

The Tuesday after my father-in-law's visitation, members of the GSA club slump into my classroom after school for their weekly meeting. They heave their backpacks onto desks as they drop into the hard seats. I can tell whether it's been a long day by the timbre of the *thud*. Most days for them are.

On this particular afternoon I am seated at the back of the room when Daniel, our club president, approaches me. "Have you heard?" he asks.

I look up from my papers. Daniel's face is grave. He tells me a student has been threatening to disrupt that afternoon's GSA meeting. "My friends and I have been texting about it all morning." Though I sometimes duck out of the classroom for a moment during meetings, I promise to stay put the entire time.

Daniel moves to the front of the room, and I return to my grading. The students—whom I can't help seeing as kids—are a baker's dozen arranged in a semi-circle. They say their names, their preferred pronouns, and, today, which Hogwarts house they'd belong to. Daniel is a Hufflepuff; he's fine with whatever pronouns.

A girl with dyed black hair and a black T-shirt sporting a print of Edgar Allan Poe's wan visage on its front says, "I'm Ray. She/

her pronouns. And I'd be a Ravenclaw." She then uses both her hands to grasp her Poe shirt and pull it forward from her body. "Quoth the raven, *evermore*, bitches," she says, eliciting some laughter from the group. I smile at the constancy of certain adolescent trends.

After introductions are finished, Daniel lays out the objectives for the meeting. "Today, we're gonna start by testing our knowledge of LGBTQ history." Someone in the back groans at the mention of a "test." I catch Daniel's eye and offer a sympathetic smile, *Welcome to my world, kid*. Daniel hands each student a notecard. On the front of each is the name of a significant person or event: "Matthew Shepard" or "Stonewall," for example. On the flipside, a brief description of that person or event: "Matthew Shepard was a gay university student who was beaten, tortured, and left to die" or "the Stonewall Inn was a haven for New York City's gay, lesbian, and transgender community and site of a notorious riot following a police raid." The goal is for the group to build a timeline of significant events in LGBTQ history. Daniel models the activity by holding up his card, reading it aloud, and then laying it on the desk in front of him, explaining when he thinks it happened. Each member of the group will take a turn then, placing cards in front of or behind previous cards. Afterward, they will check their work against the actual timeline tucked in Daniel's club folder.

Amidst the bustle someone from the club leaves to use the bathroom and doesn't bother closing the door behind them. Typically, the door is shut as a deterrent against roving students poking their heads in. I look up from my work and see two boys I do not recognize standing in the doorway. One has shaggy black hair, wears an orange hoodie, a face yet unblemished by the hormones coursing through his body. He stands with a cocky sureness. The boy beside him is shorter by at least a foot, sandy-haired and freckled. He seems jittery, too many energy drinks maybe, and he keeps looking up at his friend for a cue about what to do next.

Ash, another member of the GSA, says to them, "You shouldn't be here."

"Oh yeah," says Mr. Orange Hoodie. "Thought this was a *safe* space?"

He takes a step toward her and into the room. His minion follows suit. I stand up from my desk. The boy sees me and startles. I'm six-three and bearded, but I'm also a middle-aged high school teacher in khakis and a green sweater. Not exactly a figure of intimidation. Yet he takes a step back, almost crunching his friend's toes, and takes in the room. "This just makes me sick."

"What's your name?" I say. The boys have retreated into the hall. The orange hoodie looks left, then right, ramping up to make a run for it.

"You know you're all idiots?" he says.

"How's that?" I ask.

"Cuz there's only two genders," he hollers. They bolt.

Ash slides off her desk, yells, "ASSHOLES," and slams the door.

"Easy," I say and open the door. I follow in the direction they ran, but the boys have escaped the building through a side entrance. I return to the room and ask if anyone knows the kid's identity. Someone shouts, "Yeah. Random cis het male." Daniel is doing his best to settle the group. Several are distraught. Ash knows the orange hoodie's name. He's a freshman.

"Pretty brazen for a freshman," I say.

"They're all like that this year," she says.

"Why don't we adjourn for today, huh?" I ask. Several heads nod. "If you need some time to collect yourself, you're welcome to stay as long as you like." Some wrench their backpacks from the desks and steam off. Some gather around the wooden podium at the front of the room to commiserate. I sit at my computer and compose an email to the school's administrative team. I name the boy and document what transpired.

Two days go by without a response.

I feel a twinge of despair. In some ways I'm a surrogate parent to these GSA kids, and I can't help but see Simone in every one of them. Similar to how Ritchie saw his son in the tear-streaked face of that bullied clerk. As a teacher, I want to find the part that is human within the boy who intruded on the meeting, tease it out into the light. But as a parent, I want to tear into him. I imagine Simone in the room, wonder how she would have responded to his provocations. I know he would've been even more of a menace and caused a greater disruption had I not been there. How can I protect her when I can't always be there to protect her?

On Friday, I pass the principal on my way to lunch. "Anybody get back to you yet about GSA club?" he asks. I shake my head. "I want you to know I take this seriously." I thank him and tell him to have a nice weekend. I think again about the students in the GSA club, wondering what *their* weekends will be like.

I'm still thinking about those kids in GSA club when I get home that night. The lack of administrative action. Like many schools, being LGBTQ here attracts a certain level of teasing and harassing, and many students in the group don't have supportive families. As the parent of a trans child, I worry constantly about how my daughter is being treated and how she will be received when she encounters strangers in a hostile, increasingly hateful world. My best hope is that, for all the negativity she'll encounter, she'll also find adults—teachers, mentors, civic and political leaders—willing to defend her dignity as a human being. It was precisely this hope that led me to volunteer to advise the GSA in the first place.

I hunch over my dinner, resting my weight on my elbows, and chew my food tight-lipped. My family says nothing. Afterward, while Adrienne and Simone unwind in the living room in front of a new Netflix series, I'm still in my chair at the dining room table under a pensive brow.

Simone calls to me, "Dad, what's wrong?

"What?"

"I asked you what's up, like, ten times now."

"You did? Sorry." I look down at my arms now folded across the table. "Sometimes responses are like light from a dying star. They take a little while to reach you."

"Oooo-kayyy," she says and then turns her attention back to the show.

How am I supposed to tell her about what is really on my mind? She has enough to worry about trying to make middle school as normal an experience as possible. Still, the stakes could not be higher.

I recently reconnected over Facebook with an old poet friend from Ohio. It had been a few years.

In my last correspondence with him I had promised to send an updated photograph of "Simon" holding one of the poet's books. It was to be a recreation of a photo I sent not long after "Simon's" birth. "Simon" was tucked into his baby carrier seat so that his head appeared to be sprouting from his blanket. I crouched over him with a copy of my friend's new book in my hands, opened it to the middle, and positioned it in front of his face to look like he was reading. "Simon's" eyes widened as if startled by some image formed in that constellation of words.

Adrienne snapped the picture. My friend stuck the photo to his refrigerator and joked, "People always ask about the baby boy with the large hands. I tell them, 'That's the smartest baby in the world.'" Adrienne and I never got around to posing "Simon" for a new picture. Needless to say, there was much to update my friend on.

Within a week he wrote back. He said it was nice hearing from me and that he was at work on another book. When addressing the news that "Simon" was now Simone, he was supportive, writing, "How wonderfully brave to be who she is in the world. That's not easy for anyone." Then he said something whose profundity has continued to haunt me: "My sense about her generation is that they're teaching us about gender the way my generation taught our parents about race." While we can question just how much we've learned from those lessons about race since then, it's true that Simone's generation is, at the very least, forcing a conversation about gender identity.

In 2016, the Williams Institute on Sexual Orientation and Gender Identity Law and Public Policy, an independent think tank at the UCLA School of Law, using data from the CDC's Behavioral Risk Factor Surveillance System, estimated as many as 1.4 million U.S. citizens identified as transgender: "This figure is double the estimate that utilized data from roughly a decade ago."[6] There are more people out as trans than ever before, making the concerns of trans people more difficult to dismiss.

But also implicit in my friend's comparison is the welter of violence, which accompanies the increased visibility of any group representing a significant challenge to the status quo.

In 2018, the Transgender Murder Monitoring Project updated

---

6. Andrew R. Flores et al., "How Many Adults Identify as Transgender in the United States?" The Williams Institute (2016), https://williamsinstitute.law.ucla.edu/wp-content/uploads/Trans-Adults-US-Aug-2016.pdf.

its numbers. Twenty-eight trans people were killed in the United States.[7] And the American Medical Association declared the killing of trans women an epidemic in 2019.[8]

Monday morning, an email arrives from the assistant principal. He has been tasked with investigating the matter concerning the GSA club. The assistant principal tells me he spoke with the boys who disrupted last week's meeting, both of whom insist their intent was not to be disruptive. The school has both a French Club and a cooking club, he says, but "we do not go into those clubs saying French is not a good language or that we'd rather eat fast food." The boys understand that repeating their actions could be considered harassment and bullying. He signs off with "Thanks for letting us know" and, puzzlingly, "Enjoy!" There is no further follow up with GSA members. No consequences for the boys aside from a lecture constructed from problematic analogies. In fact, the assistant principal encourages me to leave my classroom door open during meetings in case the boys decide to one day join the GSA club. I'm gobsmacked. In the past, the administrative response has consistently been supportive, whether calming the concerns of parents calling into question the observance of the National Day of Silence in April or shutting down a student putting up Straight Pride posters on random lockers.

I stare at the computer screen, trying to comprehend how these boys' actions can only be construed as harassment if they happen a second time. As if every bully deserves a warmup round. And then the valediction at the end: Enjoy! As a teacher, I

---

[7] "TMM Update Trans Day of Remembrance 2018," (2018), www.transrespect.org.
[8] "AMA adopts new policies on first day of voting at 2019 Annual Meeting," (2019), American Medical Association.

appreciate and am supportive of restorative justice, of being slow to punish a young person for an impulsive act, but in this case, the assistant principal has essentially shrugged his shoulders and let the matter slide. As a parent, I want something more punitive.

At the next meeting, the students clamor to know what administration said, what consequences have been meted out. I pull up the email, but I don't have the heart to read them anything other than a sanitized version of it. The kids frown. Their arms hang limp. I feel like I've failed them, too. How can I look into their faces, into Simone's face, and say the message from the top seems to be, "You're on your own"? I consider the alternatives: Do I push administration on this? Do I corner and admonish the boys myself? Or do I just move on until the next crisis? I'm seething, though I know rage is not the same thing as justice or fairness. And as the students know all too well, rage is the enemy of love.

From the front of the room I hear, "I'm Daniel. Any pronouns work." I look up to see the rest of the group has arranged itself in its familiar semi-circle. It's a subtle defiance, a semblance of stability in a tottering world. For the moment, they're all they have to hang onto.

SEEDS

When I graduated from college in December 1997 with a degree in English education, grades six through twelve, no full-time work was waiting for me. But there were plenty of substitute teaching jobs in the area to keep me occupied. Being a substitute teacher meant I had to take whatever work was available, regardless of grade or subject matter. I often found myself situated well outside my comfort zone. I remember how a group of first graders, already hip to the "sub game," kept trying to confuse me as to who was who and who sat where. Later, it was payback as I, quite unintentionally, left them utterly befuddled during the math lesson on dollars and cents. Even when I did land a sub job within the language arts, it often amounted to pressing PLAY on a VCR and watching the same fifty-minute stretch of video cassette tape for five consecutive hours. One time at a middle school I dozed off during my third viewing of *The Miracle Worker*. When I opened my eyes, and my vision adjusted to the windowless murk of the dim, partitioned classroom, I saw one of the students had turned in his seat and was pointing at me, laughing. I nodded at him as if to say, "Yeah, you caught me."

When the public schools let out for summer vacation, I took whatever job I could find: pizza delivery guy, video store clerk, weekends managing the till at the comic book shop. I ultimately found a job at a child and adolescent treatment center co-supervising a unit of roughly half a dozen boys aged nine to twelve. My employment only lasted through August, but it was difficult work. Their backstories were varying degrees of trauma and abuse. When a boy went into "crisis," an agitated state in which he could harm himself or others, we were trained to physically restrain the child until other staff arrived to remove him from the unit to a room where he could safely calm himself down.

I remember working a shift with Sarah, a college student majoring in social work at the university. It was a Saturday afternoon, and the sun poured through the open blinds in the commons room, bronzing the carpet, the wood-paneled walls, all the furnishings. One boy, Trevis (with an "e"), was sitting cross-legged on the floor in a T-shirt and shorts playing chess with another boy. The sky looked hazy and hot. There was no breeze. Idle trees. Sarah and I looked at each other. We felt the quiet more than we heard it. A stiffness in the neck no amount of stretching or rubbing could assuage. In that quiet stillness, we could also feel the winding up of something explosive. When Trevis suddenly scattered the game pieces with a swipe of his hand, cursing at the boy across from him for not knowing how to play, it was almost a relief. We called to Trevis, tried to stem the tide of his anger with our words, but his gaze was distant, unreasonable, beyond our reach. His arms were still swinging wildly. It ended in a basket hold. Sarah got behind him, securing his wrists in her hands and pulling his arms straitjacket tight against his body. She braced her back against the nearest wall and slid down, taking Trevis to a seated position on the floor. I secured his legs, essentially lying over his feet. "You motherfuckers!" he yelled as he tried to bend his knees and wriggle free.

"Come on, Trevis. Just calm down," I said. For a moment, I thought my words had gotten through. I still wasn't sure what had set him off. He stopped his thrashing, his torrent of profanities. The room undulated with our breathing. Then, I heard him make a noise. Like heavy furniture dragged across a room. I was still lying at his feet. As I looked up at him, he dredged all the phlegm he could collect from the back of his throat and spat it at me. The dripping mass clung to the hinge at the end piece of my glasses and hung there like a stalactite. I could not recall a time I felt more debased. But I said nothing. I continued my hold. When I moved my head, the snot jiggled like a piece of loose, slippery flesh.

Twenty-four hours later, I was back for another shift. This time Trevis and I played chess together. He was cordial and chatty, as if our previous encounter had been a fiction. I wasn't seeking an apology. I knew it wasn't personal. I just happened to be working the day he went into crisis. When he took my knight, a calculated move I did not see, he did a little dance with his spindly arms that made me smile. And I forgot about what was written on his charts in his file and saw him like any other kid: bright and funny and capable. In a life punctuated by betrayals (and worse) at the hands of adults, how important these moments. "Seed planting," a colleague friend called it. "You have to trust that what you do for kids now will yield fruit later. Even if you're not around to see it."

I carried these things, sans the basket hold, with me to my alma mater which, in the fall of 1998, had hired me to teach English there. And while I never met Trevis's analogue that first year, I did have to contend with Jack. Slouched in the back of the room in shorts falling well below his knees, a blowsy T-shirt, and backward baseball cap, Jack was a cocky and callow sophomore. He was the first, and only, student I pulled into the hallway that first fall semester.

It was after lunch. American Literature. I asked students to open their textbooks to Ralph Waldo Emerson's essay, "Nature." I remember standing in front of the class, feeling on the spot, and comparing the reading of Emerson to winter driving in Wisconsin. "You have to go slow," I said, "and pay attention. Otherwise, your mind might swerve." Several students looked over their shoulders, out the back window, into a sun-dappled September afternoon, and then turned their heads back to me. Jack, who hadn't bothered to even take out his textbook, raised his hand and, rather than wait to be called upon, said, "Does that mean Emerson will finally make sense sometime in December?" The class snickered. I ignored the comment, and my seasonally inappropriate analogy, and began going over the day's objectives. I noticed Jack mimicking my mannerisms. I stopped talking and stared at him, hoping to shame him into silence. Instead, he extended his arms outward, in a cruciform pose, and said, "What?" That did it.

"Jack, out in the hallway. Now."

I turned and left the room. Jack took a moment to gape at his peers, made a *pffff* sound, and followed me out. We stood in front of a row of lockers. He looked up at me, his brown eyes saying, "Well?"

"What's your problem, Jack?" I said. "I'm just trying to start class."

Again, he threw his arms out in a beleaguered manner and said, "I don't understand why *the man* is coming down on *me*."

I was twenty-three years old. It was hard to conceptualize myself as "the man," but he was sixteen, and I was an authority figure. "Look, I didn't take this job so I can 'come down on you.' I took it because I want to teach. And you're making that extremely difficult for me, yourself, and twenty-four of your peers."

He leaned back, looked into the room, smiled, and pointed at someone. "What's up, guy?" he said.

"Can we call a truce?" I asked. "Can you let me teach, and I'll do my best to keep 'the man' at bay?"

"Whatever," he said. "It's your show."

We returned to the classroom and, like with Trevis, began again.

Years passed, and while I never heard from Trevis again, Jack and I stayed in touch. He graduated high school, got married, and, with his wife, created a more environmentally conscious waste management company in the Chippewa Valley, which allowed for the separation of garbage, recycling, and organic material. The problem kid turned model citizen. When my family eventually switched to his service, I told him I was happy to see he was still fighting "the man." He just smiled and wagged his right index finger at me, the way we do at people who know things about us that others never will.

Jack's entrepreneurial spirit expanded to other endeavors as well. For example, he owned and operated his own painting business. The house Adrienne and I moved into in 2004 was built in 1929. Slate siding negated the need for recurring paint jobs, but the window frames were another matter. All about the house, they were cracked and chipping. And, in the case of the front windows, the wood was rotting as well and attracting a variety of birds. We'd often rap the glass to try and startle the woodpeckers who'd come by with their jackhammer beaks. The house is also two stories tall. Neither Adrienne nor I were to be trusted with a paintbrush, a paint can, and an extension ladder. So we called Jack.

He stops by a week after the GSA incident, when I am most in need of some genuine human goodness, on his way home from a job. "Been hard at it?" I ask, and then shake my head at this superfluous question. His body is speckled with evidence; his skin and clothes, down to the tops of his steel-toed boots, are paint-spattered. I can see flecks of white in his beard that have nothing to do with age.

"More or less," he says, taking a seat at our dining room table next to Simone who is still picking at her food, delaying work on a seventh-grade science project.

I clear some dinner plates out of his way. "Get you anything to drink? Water? Soda? Beer?"

"Actually, a beer sounds pretty good right now."

I grab two bottles from the fridge and twist off their caps.

"Thanks," Jack says. Adrienne and I sit down across from him. "So," he continues, "I took a look around earlier today while you were at work. We can do this, no problem."

"That's great, Jack," Adrienne says. "When can you start?"

"I can put a guy on it after the holiday, provided the weather holds." It's one week until Thanksgiving. "Otherwise we're looking at spring." I lean my bottle over the table to *clink* with his. "First thing, though," he says, "we should talk price." I pull my bottle back.

"Uh-oh. This is sounding ominous."

He swigs his beer and says, "I don't want your money." Adrienne and I look at each other. "Oh, you heard me right. If we do this job, I don't want you to pay me for it." He looks to his left, at Simone rolling a carrot across her plate with her fork tines, and says, "I want you to make a donation to some transgender organization instead." Simone freezes and then tips her head up at us. Jack had been one of the attendees at Simone's informal naming ceremony at the park three years ago. "Is that okay?" he asks. "Can we cheers to that?" He raises his bottle to us. I am still too stunned to move, so Adrienne takes the bottle out of my hand, *clinks* it against Jack's, and takes a drink.

Later, as he is leaving, I stop him by our front door. The stars are out. Tiny seeds strewn across a vast field of sky. I tell him, "I still don't know what to say."

"A 'thanks' will do."

"Thanks." I think of those GSA kids, of Simone. Some of that familiar darkness I struggle to keep at bay dissipates. "Been difficult to believe in the best of humanity recently."

"Yeah, well, you believed in me when most teachers would've just written me off." He winks and slaps my arm and adds, "Here's to sticking it to 'the man.'" He then climbs into his truck and pulls away into the night.

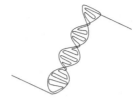

A PART OF RATHER THAN APART FROM

For Christmas 2018, Adrienne got me a 23andMe kit. She had received her genetic profile a couple years prior and had been tickled by the results. For example, she was more likely to consume larger quantities of caffeine than the average person. Not long after this revelation a rack for her coffee mugs soon appeared on our kitchen wall. Other than learning she was less Scandinavian than previously thought, there were no great surprises or health risks. Now, it was my turn to dip a toe in the gene pool. Of course, being adopted, it was a bit more complicated.

Almost a year later the kit is still wrapped in cellophane and collecting dust atop our dining room hutch. Adrienne finally says something to me the day after Thanksgiving while we trim the Yule tree. "You doing that 23andMe would be a nice gift this Christmas," she says, reaching to hang a ceramic Abominable Snowman on a branch above her head. Looking at the figurine, I can't help smiling thinking of another informative nugget yielded by her report: 23andMe's deep dive into ancestry includes Neanderthal DNA, and Adrienne's report revealed she was more Neanderthal than 67 percent of 23andMe customers.

I'm not susceptible to the conspiracy theories posited by some friends involving DNA, the government, and cloning. And despite a healthy diet of English literature warning me against probing too deeply into nature, I'm not worried about what my genes might divulge about my health. Here is a small portion of 23andMe's Terms of Service: "If your data indicate you are at an elevated genetic risk for a particular disease or condition, it does not mean you will develop the disease or condition." I'm aware of friends whose reports led to tense familial exchanges when certain geographic ancestries—and apparent infidelities—came to light. As an adopted kid, though, I can't imagine that having any bearing on my mother and father. And yet, I have put off taking the test, mostly out of nervousness. My genetic history has remained a mystery for most of my life. What clues I've been gifted over the past few years have come from seeking out, and meeting with, my birth parents. Even then, I was afforded only a surface-level understanding. What might a deeper dive disclose?

The following morning, before my body is fully awake, before I am even able to drink a glass of water, Adrienne sits me up in our bed and has me spit into a small plastic tube the kit provides. My mouth is dry and chalky. It takes a while to work up enough saliva to reach the "fill to" line on the vial. Upon hearing such strange noises coming from our room, Simone sticks her head in. "What are you guys doing in here?" she asks.

Adrienne then pops the top back on, releasing a clear liquid into my sample. She shakes the vial, commingling the contents. "That's it," she says. "Now we mail it in and wait."

For as far back as we can remember, Simone has always been Simone, even when she was "Simon." On an intuitive level, we sensed, to paraphrase Lady Gaga, maybe she was born this way, and maybe there was vindication to be found somewhere in the science, too. While listening to the Allow Me to Trans-Late podcast one weekend, I heard an interview with Dr. Alexandra Hall of the Biology Department at the University of Wisconsin-Stout. According to Hall, what constitutes biological sex, and the way it undergirds the notion that one is either male or female, is complicated by the variety we can observe in nature. She referenced intersex babies as an example. Sometimes babies are born with both ovaries *and* testes, or they have a chromosomal combination other than XX or XY, maybe XXY, or they have external genitals situating them on one end of the male/female binary, while their internal organs or hormones place them on the other end.

Regarding transgender individuals, those whose gender identities do not "match" their biological characteristics, like Simone, there have been studies done on identical twins, in which Hall noted, "[if] one of the twins is transgender, there is a twenty-five to thirty-five percent rate of the other twin also being transgender … strongly suggesting that there are genetic factors that would predispose someone."[9]

Hormones in the womb can also influence one's gender identity. Between 1940 and 1971, pregnant women were prescribed the drug Diethylstilbestrol (DES), a synthetic form of estrogen, as a means of preventing problems associated with pregnancy, like miscarriage. It didn't help. In fact, a small number of women developed cancer of the cervix and vagina before the drug was discontinued. Of those boys born to mothers whose bodies had

---

[9] Jason Soules/Dr. Alexandra Hall, "Episode Twenty-Two: Mother Nature Loves Variety," Allow Me to Trans-Late, January 2020.

been "flooded" with DES, Hall shared there was "a much higher incidence of being transgender in those male-bodied infants ... they seemed much more likely than other male-bodied infants to end up having a female gender identity brain."[10]

Speaking of the brain, Hall cited an article published in 1995 that detailed the findings of researchers who examined the brains of cadavers with varying sexual and gender identities: hetero, homo, and trans men and women. They found that the hypothalamus "tended to look one distinct way, and have a very distinct pattern, in people whose brain, their gender identity, was male and a very different way in people whose gender identity was female ... when they looked at the trans women, their brains looked exactly like the cisgendered women." This was true regardless if the trans person had undergone hormone therapy or not. Thus, she concluded, "All of the evidence we have to date suggests that there are biological causes that result in people's brains being gendered in different ways."[11]

At the end of the podcast, I felt a little better because it provided us data confirming what we've always been able to observe about Simone's life. But just because there may be a genetic component, even a predominantly genetic component, to Simone's transgender identity, it doesn't make our journey any simpler.

I wait several weeks for my results. The notification comes via email. I sit at our home computer, while Adrienne stands at my side, and click the link that will wash me back to that hormonal bath inside the womb, those deep tides of ancestral memory, a

---

10 Ibid.
11 Jason Soules/Dr. Alexandra Hall, "Episode Twenty-Two: Mother Nature Loves Variety," Allow Me to Trans-Late, January 2020.

memory I lack for I didn't grow up looking at the faces of the people I was born to. Almost immediately, Adrienne attempts to commandeer the report. "Go to your Neanderthal percentage," she says. I scroll slowly through the document, perusing each line. Adrienne huffs and takes the mouse from my hand.

"Hey," I say. "Whose information is this anyway?"

A few clicks later she exclaims, "Ha! You got 90 percent." She bumps my shoulder with her hip. "Who's the Sasquatch now?"

I hear Simone laugh from the couch across the room, her fingers frantically composing a message on her phone.

Other results are not so funny. Genes are present that indicate progressive macular degeneration as I age, as well as a risk for late-onset Alzheimer's. I think of my birth mother Lisa's father, who succumbed to Alzheimer's at the age of eighty-one. It is one thing to be cavalier when the results are merely conjecture and quite another when those results are staring me in the face. I grit my teeth and look up at Adrienne. "What about your ancestry?" she asks, changing the subject. I am predominantly French and German, which is no surprise. Again, I think of the "Family History" questionnaires filled out by both of my birth parents eight years ago. I do raise an eyebrow upon learning I have a little Greek in me. The biggest laugh is reserved for the reveal that I have the muscle composition most often seen in elite power athletes. "Maybe your dad was right," Adrienne says. "Just think if you had stuck with T-ball all those years ago."

The reading of our genes isn't always definitive. I return to 23andMe's Terms of Service: "If your data indicate that you are not at elevated genetic risk for a particular disease or condition, you should not feel that you are protected. The opposite is also true ..." Even if a genetic marker exists, environment can play a role in how, or if, that gene is eventually expressed. My report says I have the muscle composition most often seen in elite power athletes, and I chuckle at the thought of it. That has remained, shall we say, untapped.

I think of Simone, too. If she ever seeks a similar report someday, how will she read her results? Will she find she was, indeed, born with XY chromosomes? Yet what about other factors in utero: a flood of, or sensitivity to, a particular hormone, perhaps, or a brain structure anatomically different from other cisgendered boys? Dr. Hall's final thought on the Allow Me to Trans-Late podcast episode in which she was featured was as follows: "Mother nature creates this incredible diversity. That is how nature operates. If you're someone a little bit different than what may be stereotypical or 'normal' that doesn't mean there is anything wrong with you or that you're abnormal. You are valid. You are beautiful. You are whole. And you have a part in this world." Thanks to the efforts of people like Dr. Hall, there is the hope that Simone, and others like her, will be able to come of age in a culture more understanding, maybe even more nurturing, of trans people, a culture that finally sees them as a part of, rather than apart from, nature.

COMMON GROUND

Following the T-ball matchup I sabotaged as a kid by walking off the field mid-game, it was a quiet ride home with my dad at the wheel. I'm sure part of the silence was due to his processing a future without me on some court or field and without him watching from the stands. I remember thinking maybe he should have adopted some other kid. He turned onto our driveway, and I slid out of the car and went downstairs. My sister was playing video games. She invited me to join in, and I sat down beside her. The sun cast its laddered light through the half-open blinds and against the basement wall. I could hear my parents' muffled voices through the ceiling while my sister and I manipulated the trapezoidal images on the television screen via the joysticks in our hands. My father had recently purchased an Atari video game system for the family, and we had titles like *Target Fun*, *Breakout*, and *Baseball*. We simply hit the reset button whenever the game did not go our way and began again. I imagine my father pondered how to hit that reset button with me.

Now late January 2020, the winter of Simone's seventh-grade year, it's difficult to think of new beginnings. Snow is piled thigh deep outside our living room window. And yet it is a new year, the day before Simone is to travel back to Madison for puberty blockers, over eighteen months since her initial consultation, and begin the next phase of her journey. She's nervous, and I've been feeling disconnected from her. In the months since volleyball ended, we've hunkered down at home, seemingly biding our time until spring. To remedy all this, I've asked if there's something she'd like to do, just the two of us, to take her mind off tomorrow, to reconnect. She is sitting cross-legged on the couch and says, as if she's been waiting her whole life for me to ask this question: "I want to get a mani-pedi with you, Dad."

From across the room, Adrienne coughs in her chair, and I know it is cover for her laughter.

I was not expecting this, so I initially resist the idea. I suggest I try braiding her hair instead, or we re-watch *Toy Story* together.

Simone looks up, and her eyes pin me like an insect to the wall. "You said you wanted to do something I want to do. Be spontaneous, Dad."

I sigh and think of my father.

Growing up, it was easier for me to connect with my mother than with him. He often sequestered himself in his workshop in the basement, leaving my patient mother alone to listen to my childish ruminations. Depending on my mood, her lap was either the perfect psychologist's couch or church confessional.

That's not to say my dad didn't try to reach out. During the peak of Nancy Reagan's "Just Say No" anti-drug campaign in the 1980s, my father awkwardly sat on the edge of my bed, moments before lights out, asking if everything was okay, if I needed to talk about anything, oh, and was I taking any drugs?

"Uh, no, Dad," I said. He patted my leg through the covers and said, "Good," before catching the light switch on his way out the door.

It would be many years before I'd come to understand that sports were just another way my father hoped to reach out to me. When that didn't work, he found other ways to meet me where I was. There was no pressure for me to return to the T-ball team or, in time, to join any other team. And I'm sure he was experiencing a range of emotions: disappointment, embarrassment, and some small amusement when he drove me down the hill to Kerm's, a neighborhood grocery store, one day and stood off to the side while I spun the book kiosk and took in the lurid paperbacks.

"This one," I said. "Right here."

I had selected the novelization of an upcoming film epic: *Friday the 13th Part VI: Jason Lives*. The cover was cobalt blue, crawling with lightning, a decomposed hand gripping a blood-tipped machete in the foreground, the iconic hockey mask in the background. It would be confiscated by a disapproving teacher later that fall.

My father smiled and shrugged his shoulders. "Okay."

That summer, I somehow convinced my dad to take me to see *Friday the 13th Part VI: Jason Lives* at the Gemini Drive-In. Mom didn't need to know. It would be our dark secret. The screen blazed with menace as dusk dropped and spread like black ink off a painter's brush. We sat in his conversion van, radio tuned in as the sound was better than the vintage speakers fastened to the poles beyond our windows, the cool digital blue of the clock lighting our faces from below, munching popcorn while mostly missing our mouths. I did glance at him once, to smile.

And so, I've come now to inhabit my father's role, to be open to whoever my kid turns out to be, and rather than an adoptive dad, be an adaptive dad, instead. After considering her ultimatum, Simone and I are bundled up and mall-bound, destined for the nail boutique. But a day at the nail boutique is not a day at the movies. On the way there I keep side-glancing at Simone. "I don't know about this," I say. "What if it hurts?" I am purposefully playing up my worry, knowing she is taking some small joy in my affected reluctance, but there is real reluctance, as well. Unlike braiding her hair or sitting beside her to watch some Pixar flick, this will leave a mark. Before we left home, Simone made it clear that my toenails and fingernails would indeed be painted and in a color she got to pick. Adrienne asked what color she was thinking. I thought of my students, my colleagues, the strangers at the gym, and inwardly cringed. Simone said, "Some color you can see from outer space."

Upon arrival, we shiver out of our winter coats and are welcomed by a young woman dressed in black asking what we would like. I scan the room. A few women are having their nails done. No other men at this time. I look at Simone, who looks at me like I'm supposed to know what to do. "Um," I stammer, "a mani." The woman nods. The words feel alien on my tongue. "And a pedi."

She tells us to select the color polish we desire and to have a seat along the wall. There is a row of chairs with small basins for our feet. Simone grabs a bottle from the display case: a fleshy tone, like the skin of a peach, almost the color of the nail itself. I relax. Perhaps no one will notice after all.

"This one's for me, Dad, and this ..." She hands a bottle to me. "is for you." I hold it up to the light like a film negative.

"Blue," I say. "With sparkles." I hear her giggle, and it's scratched with mischief.

We hang our coats on hooks, take off our shoes and socks, and roll up our pant legs. We sit next to each other, and Simone informs me that our chairs have a massage option. We press the power buttons on the remote controls attached to the right arms of the chairs. Simone says to next click the "kneading" button.

There is an immediate sensation in my lower back muscles as if some clog-wearing centipede is dancing a waltz along my spine. Meanwhile, the woman attending to my feet produces a slender, metal tool with a curved head, like something a dentist might use to remove tartar buildup from my teeth, and proceeds to dig around underneath my toenails. I wince a bit and see Simone smirking at me.

Next up is the pumice stone. It tickles as it grates over the most sensitive parts of the bottoms of our feet. Simone bites her lip before caving into a belly laugh, which makes the woman at her feet laugh, too.

The women then squirt lotion into their hands to moisturize our feet. They speak to each other in their native tongue while they work. The scent of menthol and a whiff of citrus soothes. They cover our legs and feet with hot towels before a soft divider is placed between our toes, and they finally begin painting.

I feel my phone buzz in my pants pocket and retrieve it. It's my dad. These days he always seems to call at the most inopportune times. I say to Simone, "I gotta take this."

"Dad," she whines. "It's supposed to be our day, remember?"

"It's your grandpa, and it's still our day." I answer the call. "Hello? Dad?"

"It's thirty-one degrees out," he says. I imagine him at home in his recliner, dividing his attention between the television before him and the weather clock on the countertop next to him.

"Yeah," I say, "Balmy. What's up?"

"I need more ... things."

"Things?" These guessing games have become more common.

"You know," he says, "that you put in your mouth."

"Groceries?"

"Yeah."

Simone looks at me, her eyes pleading with me to get off the phone so that I don't miss key details of the experience. I hold up my index finger to her. "Well, I won't be able to grab them for you until later tomorrow. We're off to Madison in the morning for an appointment."

"That's okay," he says.

"Guess what I'm doing now?" I watch Simone's toenails change color. "Getting my nails done with Simone."

There is silence, and then he says, "Oh boy."

I put the phone down and compliment Simone on her choice. I hear my dad call my name then, and it sounds distant, like out of a dream, the one in which, try as I might, I'm unable to reach him. Yet here he is on the line, lucid and chatty, beyond the fog of his dementia, and though it's a day out with my daughter, the eve of her whole world changing, I can't let him go just yet. "I'm here, Dad." I keep watching Simone and think about how it took becoming a father to realize how much my dad did push beyond traditional notions of parent-child relationships. "And I want to thank you," I say, fidgeting in my chair, careful not to disturb the woman working on my feet. "For preparing me to be a parent all those years ago. Even if I didn't recognize it at the time we were sitting in those theaters."

No response. For a second I fear a lost connection, and then he says, "We sure saw some weird movies, didn't we?"

I smile. "Yeah, we did." I hesitate a moment before adding, "And I love you for that, Dad."

"It's thirty degrees out now," he says. "And dropping."

"I know, Dad. I promise to keep warm. I'll call you when I get back from Madison."

"Okay."

I hang up, tuck the phone into my pocket, and relax back into my chair. "No more distractions," I say to Simone.

"Took you long enough."

I think of the words I just exchanged with my father. "It sure did," I say.

Our feet are finished, and it's time to move on to our hands. With socks and shoes, toes can be discreet. Not so with fingernails. I imagine mine as a beacon burning so brightly at the end of their elongated digits they will be seen from anywhere in town pulsing like radio antennae along the horizon.

We put on thin, yellow sandals, like walking on paper, and move to a series of tables set up in the middle of the room. Simone is seated at the table behind me. I take my place next to a woman whose nails are also being painted. As my fingers are prepped, my attendant asks if I am sure about this. Her eyes seem to say there's no shame in bowing out. I look back at Simone, who meets my gaze and smiles, so happy. I think of the Gemini Drive-In with my father, still vivid, cosseted in my memory. "This is what she wants," I say. "Let's do it."

The woman next to me says, "At least it's not pink."

I say, "She knows blue is my favorite color."

"Much more a manly color," the attendant says. It seems the binary of his or hers is cross-cultural.

"Especially with sparkles," I say.

The first layer goes on, a cyan blue. *Not so bad*, I think, and yet I ask how long I will have these nails.

"A few days, usually," the attendant says.

There is an expiration of acetone as she uncaps the bottle she will use for the sparkle effect. She gently layers it over the top of each finger. When the light catches my nails just right, they shimmer and look like how bumping your funny bone feels.

She finishes and guides me to another table. There are white lamps for my hands and feet above and below it. She instructs me to place my hands and feet beneath these ultraviolet nail curing lamps to dry the polish. I am to sit here for fifteen minutes.

There is time to think of how I, too, have become, like my father, something of a basement dweller of late: occupied with my work, watching one too many movies on our big screen. It was my dad who finished our basement for us. I carried rectangles of sheetrock down to him, the truly masculine moments so few and far between in my life, and inadvertently ended up walling myself in like poor Fortunato in Poe's "The Cask of Amontillado." Yet here was Simone ready to break down walls, again.

"So what do you think, Dad?"

I look at my hands under the lamp's purple glow. "Feeling cute," I say. "Might delete later."

Her mouth drops open, and she sucks in a breath of surprise at my referencing the trendy social media meme. "How do you know about that saying?"

I play it cool. "Your dad knows a few things."

It is as if she is seeing me for the first time as someone other than just her dad, and I bask in it before reminding her it's still me.

"I am wondering, though," I say, looking down at my fingers. "How am I supposed to pick my nose now?"

"Dad, please don't ruin the moment."

As a kid, it was easy for me to blame whatever distance was present between my dad and me on the fact I was adopted. In spite of my hair getting longer and each of the heavy metal T-shirts I wore being more alienating than the last, in spite of my phantom jealousy of the "deeper" conversations concerning sports my father seemed to have with my friends and could not have with me, it was a convenient chip to carry on my adolescent shoulders. But rather than take me to a stadium, my dad continued to find time to take me to the movies. We saw Mary Lambert's adaptation of Stephen King's *Pet Sematary*. We were there opening night for both Sam Raimi's *Darkman* and Tom

CLUMSY LOVE

Savini's underappreciated remake of George Romero's *Night of the Living Dead*. As it turns out, the dimmed confine of a movie theater was the perfect place for us. My father and I have never been ones to hug it out or talk it out, and once the lights went low, the curtains drew back, and the Dolby digital thundered, there was no time for that anyway.

Maybe the nail boutique is the perfect place for Simone and me. When my time is up underneath the ultraviolet light, we both get ready to leave. I am surprised by the sudden care I feel toward my nails. They are delicate blue shells that glisten in the store light. I don't want to smudge this woman's beautiful work. I slowly slide my arms through my coat sleeves. Simone is pleased with hers, too, looking back at me and flashing her hands for effect. I flash mine back and smile at her. However, once we leave the store, it doesn't take long for those gendered fears to return. I'm hardly a poster boy for masculinity, but the nails make me suddenly self-conscious. I pass a man wearing a backward ball cap and a gray Affliction T-shirt. He notices my nails, and I want to bury my hands deep into my coat pockets. I look at Simone walking in front of me, and I am pricked by a small sliver of empathy for what it must feel like to be her every moment of every day. Though in a matter of time, a week maybe, according to the attendant, all evidence of my social transgression will be history: chipped, flaked, dissolved away. If someone happens to call me out beforehand, I can always laugh it off as "something you do for your daughter." I can walk away from this experiment with little to no scathing. Not so for Simone. The least I can do is leave my naked hands at my side. And so I do. The man continues on without a word. Another non-incident. I know I may never be able to fully bury my suspicion of my fellow human, but I also know now I can rise above it. Beacon be damned.

ESCAPE ARTISTS

At thirteen years old, Simone feels puberty counting down like the timer in an escape room. And she is determined to avoid an ineluctable fate: the onset of maleness. The paint on our nails has barely dried from the day before when we hop in the car and head for Madison, once again to the PATH Clinic, for a procedure that will block male puberty in Simone. The procedure itself will only take twenty minutes; however, its ramifications will prove resonant for years to come. It is a decision we have not entered into lightly.

The drug is histrelin acetate, a gonadotropin-releasing hormone (GnRH) analogue, which will be implanted into Simone's left bicep and last for two years. An incision, roughly the size of a staple, is made in the arm, and the medicine is inserted within. The medicine was developed to remedy what is known as "precocious puberty," or puberty that begins at an unusually early age, for example, five years old. It is commonly used in cases of gender nonconformity as well. The risks are minimal. It's what comes after, though, that has filled our heads with questions and concerns: the requisite hormonal therapy, the eventual gender reassignment surgery, Simone's acceptance as a woman by others. Andrew Solomon writes, "People often question a trans person's authenticity in his or her affirmed gender."

For Simone's part, she has not wavered in the slightest over the past year and a half since our last visit. If anything, her conviction has grown stronger, bolstered, no doubt, by the ticking of her own biological clock. Gender aside, it's hard not to think about the cumulative loss of the past year, the deaths of both her grandmother and grandfather, and wonder if it has contributed in some small way to the intensification of her desire to apply the brakes and remain a child a bit longer.

To be fair, there is some fear on her part, the kind of trepidation any escape artist must feel when facing whatever feat lays before them, be it a straitjacket, a water tank, or puberty. She worries about the pain. She imagines the whole of her arm being cut open, of bearing witness to the inner mechanism of her muscle laid bare and wet and red. And so we have tried to make the journey as comfortable and distracting as possible. It is hardly the auspicious start we hoped when, thirty minutes into the trip, she realizes she forgot to charge her electronic devices. "Why didn't you guys check when you got up this morning?" Simone asks. Adrienne is driving, and I can tell she is repressing the urge to lecture Simone on responsibility. Besides, it will only end with Simone reminding us we aren't the ones getting our arm cut open.

The sun is out, and the roads are clear of snow. We arrive at the PATH Clinic shortly after one in the afternoon. The friendly receptionist and the aquarium teeming with fish in the waiting area all feel familiar and welcoming. We shed our outer garments and wait. When Simone's name is called, a nurse greets us and ushers us through a door and runs Simone through a series of protocols recording weight, height, and answers to questions like the reason for our visit. She then leaves us in a room, and we wait for the doctor.

Soon there is a knock on the door. A woman peeks her head in. "Hello," she smiles and introduces herself. She is a different doctor from the one we met with on our previous visit. Her hair is pulled back into a ponytail, a white lab coat over a casual blouse and slacks. She sits down at the desk next to us and pushes what looks like a plate of flesh-colored jello toward Simone.

"What's that?" Simone asks, watching it wobble.

"That," she says, pausing for effect, "is an arm."

Simone recoils from it.

"It's not a real arm," the doctor says. "Here. Touch it."

Simone is hesitant, wondering if this is some sort of trick, looking to Adrienne and me to tell her what to do. She then reaches out and wiggles the wrinkled mound. "Cool," she says, genuinely surprised.

The doctor takes Simone's hand and focuses it on a particular spot. "Feel that?" she asks.

Simone nods.

"That is what the implant will feel like once it's in your arm."

While Simone continues to massage the spot, the doctor asks if we have any questions about the procedure before she begins. Simone asks if it will hurt.

"We have a numbing shot for that." Simone reacts to the mention of a shot. "Honestly," the doctor adds, "that's the hardest part. Waiting for you to numb up takes longer than placing the implant. What else is on your mind?"

"Are you going to cut my arm open?" Simone asks.

The doctor grabs a pen and makes three horizontal dashes on a piece of paper. "That's how big the implant is. So that's about how big the incision is going to be."

The reassurance from this higher authority seems to work. "Okay. I'm ready."

Simone climbs up on the examination table and lies back so that her head rests on the pillow and her body ruffles the paper beneath. The doctor tells her it's okay for one of us to stand by her side and hold her right hand. To my surprise, she asks for me. I take my spot at Simone's side and squeeze her hand in mine. I smile at our new nails and think how, unlike at the mall, no one here has noticed or cared. I think, too, of the last time I held her hand when we were here for X-rays charting her bone growth. How tiny and childlike it felt then.

The doctor swabs Simone's left bicep with alcohol. Simone tenses a bit and grasps my hand harder. She is pondering only the pain, while I am pondering the implications of that pain. Sensing Simone's concern, the doctor pauses before injecting the numbing agent. She gets Simone talking about what's going on in her life instead. Simone struggles to think of a response.

"What about Girls Rock Band?" Adrienne asks.

"Girls Rock Band? What's that?"

"It's through the music school," Simone says. "There's six of us, and we play shows at coffee shops, museums, places like that." When volleyball season ended, Simone picked up a new extracurricular, performing in the all-girls rock band RAAD BEANZ (short for "rad human beings"). Their first gig was at the Shift Cyclery and Coffee Bar in downtown Eau Claire on a Sunday evening. Afterward, Adrienne and I got in line for a signed poster of the event. Simone was seated with her bandmates behind a wooden table in the cyclery portion of the shop, where a couple bikes hung over their heads. She was grinning as they wrote their names and flashed peace signs for their parents' phones.

"Cool," the doctor says. "And what do you play?"

"I sing," Simone says.

"And what do you sing?"

"Well, the last song I sang was Katy Perry's 'Roar.'"

"Not sure if I know that one," the doctor says. "Do you think you could sing it for me?"

"I'll try. Never sang it lying down before."

The room fills with the sound of Simone's sweet voice. A couple nurses in the vicinity crack open the door and stick their heads in. When the song is finished, there is light applause. "Wow," the doctor says. "What a great voice. I was not expecting that."

Simone smiles. "Thank you."

"Are you feeling relaxed now?" the doctor asks.

Simone nods.

"Good. I'm going to numb your arm up, okay? You might feel some pressure." She slips the needle in. Simone looks at the ceiling, the wall, me, and then the needle comes out. "Hard part's over," the doctor says and steps out of the room for a moment to give the shot time to take effect.

When Simone's arm is ready, the doctor returns and prepares to make the cut for the implant. There is some small talk between them, but I'm not listening. I am thinking, *This is it. This commitment is for real.* The past and the future begin to shift before my eyes like a mirage or a fever dream. I watch her laying there, and for a moment her hair recedes to the length it was when she was "Simon," and I can see him in his gold fairy wings, impervious to the world. And then the hair grows back, and she is Simone again, only she is older now, on her way to her first hormone therapy.

"Dad." Simone's voice cuts through to the present. "We're done."

The doctor is applying Steri-Strips to the incision and then wraps a pressure bandage around Simone's arm. She instructs us to keep the bandage on for twenty-four hours to minimize the bruising. The strips can come off in three days. The implant should encyst in her arm during that time. Meanwhile, Simone must avoid any vigorous activity. "Does this mean I get out of gym class?" she asks.

The doctor laughs and says, "I think you'll be okay. Just be mindful of your arm."

"Darn," Simone says.

The doctor reminds us the implant is good for two years, at which point Simone will need to swap out the old one for a new one. Simone will also need to start hormone treatments within two years or risk bone health and brain development. "Noted," I say.

"I'm very happy to have met you, Simone," the doctor says. "You're very brave. Like the song says: we're going to hear you roar. Good luck."

On the car ride back to Eau Claire, we ask Simone if she feels any different. "Not really. It's more peace of mind. I was worried my voice was starting to change."

"You mean get lower?" Adrienne asks.

"Uh-huh."

Suddenly, we are a chorus of voices attempting to get as low as we can in our respective registers. I bellow a line from that Katy Perry song, and Simone laughs, "Stop, Dad." It's a moment of levity that allows my brain a break from the worries of the future. When I asked the doctor how long puberty blockers were necessary, she said indefinitely—unless Simone elected for gender reassignment surgery someday. When Adrienne asked about the physical risks associated with estrogen treatments, the doctor said blood clots, weight gain, and associated comorbidities. At the same time, I considered the social risks, including potential rejection by other women and the judgment (or worse) from men. So I listen to Simone's caricature of a baritone in the back seat, and it doesn't strike me as irrational to want to keep her within arm's reach for all time.

I think of my mother and the moment I understood, whether it was the simulated violence on a movie screen or the actual violence of a ravaging disease, that she would never stop protecting me. The irony, of course, is that she couldn't shield me any better than I could hide my guilt from her as a child or that Adrienne and I can deflect some stranger's staring at Simone. As parents, we build structures to shield our children from the realities of the world. But the world's realities are a straight-line wind destined to rip the roof from those structures. Yet what is love if not a parent's body taking as much of that slashing rain and nicking debris as it can stand?

AN ENDING-BEGINNING

Despite my being a teacher, Simone rarely asks for my help with schoolwork. Adrienne is her go-to guide through the esoterica of middle school mathematics. However, Simone comes to me whenever she has to write something, say, a story for English class.

We are en route to West Bend to visit Adrienne's mother, Karen, on the eve of her selling the family restaurant. It's late February, a month after our visit to the PATH Clinic, a month since Simone started on puberty blockers, and so far, so good. Adrienne is driving the Sienna, and I am riding shotgun. Simone is in the back seat and casually slides her laptop over the cup holder island and onto my knees. She has been tasked with writing a fictional piece in collaboration with another kid in her class. She wants me to read both her and her friend's contributions. She tells me it's a post-apocalyptic tale in the style of *Alita: Battle Angel*, a film they have both recently watched and adored.

I pick up the laptop, and Adrienne says, "Your fingernails."

"So much for it being gone after a few days," I say. I turn my left hand and admire the nail salon attendant's blue sparkled handiwork from my father-daughter outing with Simone the previous month.

"Dad," Simone moans from behind me. "Read."

Her friend's section is first and focuses on the inner conflicts of the main character. Simone's section is more outward looking, allowing readers to see the character in physical action with other characters. Given their contrasting styles, the story coheres remarkably well. Simone watches me read every page. She is seeking validation, an affirmation she is "doing it right." She is also thirteen years old. Some of what she has written is indeed a kind of forgery, with names and locations changed, but much of what I wrote at her age was an imitation of stories I loved. And some of her word choice is striking. What it lacks is an ending. I settle on the middle ground of vague praise and a gentle nudge toward revision. "You handle action scenes really well, Simone, but your story sort of just stops."

"That's because it's an ending-beginning." She says this with such surety, like it's something every writer should recognize. She studies me then, as if seeing me in a new light, as someone whose credibility has suddenly come into question. "You've never heard of an ending-beginning?" she asks. I wait for her explanation. "It's when the story finishes, but you know there's more story to tell." So she wants to leave her story open-ended. I do not correct her, though. In fact, I kind of like her oxymoronic phrasing. As one story ends, another begins.

It has been many months now since my mother died, yet I dream about her almost every night. Sometimes she shows up only for a moment, or when she has no good reason to. Like when I dreamed I was running late to teach my first-hour class. I was coming out the door when she and my dad pulled up in a car to give me a ride to work. Her face was no longer gaunt, her eyes bright with the morning light. And my father was driving again, certain of the way, heading toward, not away from, me this time. As anxiety dreams go, this one was pretty anodyne. I am grateful it allowed for a bit more time with her, even if it was all inside my head. I do not believe I am in communion with the dead or that my mother is reaching out to me from beyond the grave. In my waking life, I am still grieving her loss, and lately, I've been writing about her, so I am not surprised when residual thoughts of her reveal themselves in my dreams. It's an opportunity to thank her once again for the gift of my life.

My birth mother was fifteen years old when she had me. I remember staring into the faces of my freshmen students that first year I taught high school, trying to imagine any of those fifteen-year-old girls as mothers. I couldn't. Many were still baby-faced themselves. And so, I was put up for adoption. Two months later, Rick and Judy Patrie, the only parents I've ever known, brought me to the only home I've ever known in Eau Claire, Wisconsin, where I continue to live and work and have a family of my own. Growing up, I never asked why my parents sought adoption. The question always seemed impertinent. A chance at a life had been given to me. No need to ask why. The reason eventually came to light, though: my father's infertility, which confirmed my earlier decision not to go prying. As a Catholic couple, I'm sure they grieved their inability to procreate. But I was also astonished by their conviction. They were so certain they wanted a child that nothing, not even biology, could prevent it. However, when it came time for Adrienne and me to expand our family, I wasn't so certain I wanted a child.

ANDREW PATRIE

A friend once told me, "Andy, there are three things you're never ready for in life: getting married, buying a house, and having kids." She was right about the kids. I knew I was emotionally ready to marry Adrienne. It was merely a question of timing. When Adrienne and I grew sick of renting, we knew buying a home was something we could afford. But making a kid from scratch and then raising and sustaining it? We seemed to have a good thing going just the two of us. No need to interrupt it. Over dinner at a downtown restaurant one November evening, Adrienne told me, in no uncertain terms, "Having children isn't negotiable." By December she was pregnant.

The whole time the baby was in utero, I worried about it, about Adrienne, sure, but also about what came after the birth. The responsibility was scary. Kids are transient beings in our lives. I think of my students. Every September they show up. Come June, they are gone. It's a cycle of attachment/detachment. In the meantime, we fill their heads with as much information as we can to prepare them for a life beyond us. Will we do the job as well as, or, in some cases, better than our predecessors? Much of this concern melts away the moment the students walk through the door, and we are off and running, too busy with the daily realities to ponder such matters. And this was also true the moment I first held "Simon" in my arms. The worry became less about how I was doing and more about how he was doing. That hasn't changed today, only now the worry is how Simone is doing. In a sense, Adrienne and I have had to adopt a child, too. Like my parents, we've had to reimagine what family means, what family looks like, and learn to love the kids we didn't expect to have.

CLUMSY LOVE

Back in the car, Simone seems satisfied with my critique of her work. We soon arrive at Adrienne's parents' restaurant a little after dark. The parking lot is packed, and we have to hunt for a spot. "Not bad for its final run," I say. In the months after Adrienne's father, Bob, died, the restaurant had become an unwieldy proposition for Karen, so she decided to sell it. This is the last night that Walden: A Supper Club will be in operation. Tomorrow afternoon there will be a customer appreciation event to deplete the leftover booze. Then, new ownership takes over. One story ends, another begins.

It's a bittersweet weekend for sure. Adrienne is saying goodbye to another piece of her father. And Karen, a former teacher, has invested over thirty years in this place. When Adrienne and I first started dating, I came here to visit and meet her parents. Bob and Karen gave us a private booth in the back of the dining area. The seat was a semi-circle, and Adrienne and I entered at opposite ends, scooting closer until we met in the middle. I made a *Lady and the Tramp* comment to break the tension, and Adrienne laughed. I knew then our relationship would last.

"I think this might be the last stall," Adrienne says, maneuvering the Sienna between two cars. The headlights freeze on the vehicle parked directly in front of us. We all gape at the audacious bumper sticker adhered to the lower right corner of the tailgate: "Black Trucks Matter." It's a deflating moment, for sure.

"That's racist," Simone says.

I flash my fingernails at Simone and say, "Wait until this crowd gets a load of me." A bit of humor to salve the pain.

Simone waits a beat before flashing her pink-polished fingernails at me. "Until they get a load of us, Dad."

In the past I would have followed up her statement with something like, "Us against the world, kid," and gone for a fist bump. But, in spite of my clumsy parenting over the years, she has always been out in the world, and for the first time, she is feeling at home in her own skin, not an outcast from it, which also makes me feel at home in my own skin. This family is where I fit in. As she places her laptop into her backpack, I marvel at how much she has taught me, how I've come to appreciate fatherhood/parenthood in more capricious and generous ways as a result of our journey with Simone. I lean my head back toward her and say, "I'm lucky to have you in my life. To be your dad, I mean."

Simone gives me a sympathetic look before saying, "Yes, you are." I laugh and look down at the floor. She smiles. "Let's get going before you make this more awkward."

I open my car door and step into the night. The air temperature is unseasonably warm. Sign of an early spring. Adrienne has already gone on ahead to find her mother. I stretch and wait for Simone. A breeze shakes a sentinel of pines along the property line. I have an impulse to take Simone by the hand and safely guide her through the parking lot, but she has already floated on, like a bubble blown through a plastic wand, toward the neon blaze of the "Open" sign in the restaurant's front window. There is a womanly confidence to her movement, and I think, she is my daughter, both a child and not a child, or at least not a child for very much longer. A half-moon is alight in the sky above us. I mark its position, get my bearings, and follow after her.

ACKNOWLEDGMENTS

There are plenty of people who deserve recognition and thanks for the book you now hold in your hands. As I write these words, it's been five years since I finished a first draft of *Clumsy Love*. It took me ten months of intermittent basement dwelling to do it. But I wasn't alone. David McGlynn was never more than a text message away to offer reassurance, advice, or a pep talk, and Adrienne Walden taped notecards to my computer monitor with messages like "You're writing a book!" to keep me going. Not sure I'd have finished without your faith in me and the story. I'm indebted to you both.

Other debts I'll probably never be able to repay include the following people who read early (and sometimes subsequent) drafts and offered invaluable feedback along the way: BJ Hollars, Eric Rasmussen, Ken Szymanski, Riley Drake, Allyson Loomis, and Leo Macallan.

Justin Patchin, Julian Emerson, Lindsey Brandrup, and Jeff DeGrave also deserve praise for their insights on a few individual chapters I shared at our monthly writers' group.

Shout out to Jason Splichal and *Sky Island Journal*, *Barstow and Grand*, Nick Meyer and all at *Volume One* magazine, and Erika Janik and Maureen McCollum and all at Wisconsin Public Radio for publishing embryonic versions of some of these chapters.

ANDREW PATRIE

A thousand "thank yous" to Kristin Mitchell and Shannon Booth at Little Creek Press for believing in the book and helping to get it out to the world.

Cheers to UW-Health and Mayo Clinic Health Systems, Bob Nowlan, Jodi Emerson, Maggie Ginsberg, Chippewa Valley Writers' Guild, Dotters Books, the Eau Claire Public Library, Julie Lepp and UUC, Cory Crowell and Nate Kitzrow and the Savage Horror Creeps podcast, Jason Soules, Zach and Jamie Pappas, Tyler Bee and family, Bruce Weigl, my dear friends and family including Rachel Christiansen, Ari Anand, Ana DeGrave, Corey Carrell, Dave and Paulette Sampson, Brian Strabel, Andy and Heidi Fisher, Adam and Katie Keeton, Stan and Joni Nesbit, Harold and Kattis House, Chad Lewis and Nisa Giaquinto, Linda and Bob Baker, Kara Travis and family, Kevin and Jill Dawson, Craig and Mary Brenholt, John and Nancy Nielsen, Karen and Karrin Walden, Nikki, Jim, Caleb, Campbell, and Jett Ebben, all my colleagues and students past and present, and, of course, Simone Patrie: I love you.

Finally, I'd like to acknowledge the people I lost as I was working through that first draft of *Clumsy Love*: my father-in-law Robert "Bob" Walden, my good friend Christian Grottke, and my beloved mother Judy Patrie (soon followed by my father Richard Patrie). All those notebooks you bought me as a kid so I could fill them with my stories finally paid off, Mom and Dad, and I wish you were both still around to read this one.

An early version of "Follow Your Path" was originally published in *Barstow and Grand* Issue Three Fall 2019 as "In Our Own Time."

An early version of the second part of "What Would You Do?", the birthday at the waterpark scene, was originally published in *Sky Island Journal* Issue One Summer 2017 as "Common Ground."

An early version of the latter part of "Simone," the hotel pool scene, was originally broadcast on Wisconsin Public Radio's

Wisconsin Life series on October 26, 2016 as "Simone, a Parent's Story."

A truncated version of the "Dad jokes" section in "I Sing the Body Telekinetic" was originally published in *Volume One Magazine*'s April 10, 2021 issue as "Balancing the Universe, One Dad Joke at a Time."

An early version of "Visiting Hours" was originally published in *Sky Island Journal* Issue Six Fall 2018.

A truncated version of "Seeds" was originally published in *Volume One Magazine*'s September 8, 2022 issue as "Planting Seeds for Tomorrow."

ANDREW PATRIE

ABOUT THE AUTHOR

Andrew Patrie teaches English language, literature, and creative writing in West Central Wisconsin where he lives with his family. He has self-published two previous collections of poems: *Nights, Grace* (2006) and *Half-Life* (2016). His work has appeared most recently in *Barstow and Grand, Sky Island Journal, Twig,* and on Wisconsin Public Radio. He is a contributor to *Volume One* magazine and the underground Polish heavy metal 'zine Burning Abyss. *Clumsy Love* is his first nonfiction book.

CLUMSY LOVE

Printed in the United States
by Baker & Taylor Publisher Services